A GUITARIST'S GUIDE TO THEORY

WHAT YOU NEED TO KNOW TO BECOME A BETTER MUSICIAN.

Bryan DeLauney

Table of Contents

A special thanks to http://jguitar.com/ for allowing me to use their scale diagrams and chord charts!!

Go visit their site, its great!

Chapter 1
Introduction

Too many times I have heard, "I don't get it". I hear that, or have heard that from most guitarists when discussing theory. Even when I am the instructor I get to hear that phrase on a regular basis. I encourage students to use a pen and a piece of paper to write things down, but they never listen. Now when you have read a majority of this, you will understand why I say to write things down.

Theory takes away the guesswork in music. Why do some scales sound good over certain chords and others don't? What scale can I play over a certain chord progression? What is a key? How do I know what chords to use? What in the world is a Cmin7b5? What is the difference between major and minor? These can all be answered in this book, plus many other questions.

There is too much information in music for one to just store it in virtual memory. When there are so many different scales and modes, it helps to refer back to a piece of paper to visualize things. The vision helps to lock things into memory and writing things down is also a memory tool. Use a pen and paper.... For real. No joke.

Now let's talk about music. I do understand that most people will brush over the introduction like it is a waste of time, and get on with the cool stuff, but just give me a minute to get the ball rolling. Use this book as a reference, guide, tool, kindling, torch, I don't care really. But, if you want to get something out of music you need to know that music is, not how many notes you can play a second, it's not how cool you are, it isn't how smart you are, nor is it how many scales you can memorize.

Music is in the mind, it is a rhythm, a melody. All of the scales in the world will make you a better nobody, but using one scale wisely will make you a star. Practice and study is the key. When you start a new section, understand it fully before you move on. When you play a new scale or mode, don't just memorize it and move to the next one. Put on a jam track and try to use it. Integrate it into your playing and go from one scale that you know into the new scale you just learned. Do that before you move on and it will come together more smoothly.

Claude Debussy said wisely, "Music is the space between the notes". I happen to agree with that statement. Don't get me wrong, I like to shred too, but there is more to music than fast, long runs. Try to embellish notes with overly dramatic bends, slides, reverse bends, vibrato, and timing. Every note doesn't have to be 1/16 or 1/8. Try holding notes for longer periods than you would normally and see how they sound. Record your practices and listen to them. Hear your mistakes before others do.

This book doesn't teach what a bend is or how to tune your guitar. This book is about theory and how to use your brain. This book isn't about "licks", but about how to overcome the stumbling block of knowledge. I want you to come away from this understanding theory and not be afraid of it. I have heard many guitarists say that theory wasn't important, yet they didn't know the difference between an A minor and a coal miner.

This book is not intended to be a stand alone, learn it all, and know everything kind of book. There is so much involved in music theory that people get doctorates in the subject. There is no way I can cover that level in one book. This book should coincide either with prior knowledge and/or lessons. The fundamentals of theory are not difficult. They aren't exceptionally easy, nor are they insanely unlearnable. Take your time. You don't have to read this book in a day. Take small bites, work hard, study, use your pen and paper, ask your instructor or someone who knows (email a music professor) if you have questions, and enjoy yourself. You play a guitar not work a guitar. Make it fun.

I usually get the question on if I have the knowledge, how do I apply it. The key to knowledge is understanding. Having knowledge is useless unless you understand the knowledge you possess. I have decided to insert a section at the end of chapters on how to use what has been learned from that chapter. It won't be exhaustive, but may give you an idea on why you just worked so hard.

Take the time to see the relationships between scales, keys, chords, etc. How do these chords relate? How do these three chords in this chord pattern relate to the notes in the scale playing over them? The take home lesson here is relationships. Look at the notes. Compare notes in chords. Compare notes in scales. Compare notes from scales to chords.

Let's get started learning!!!

Chapter 2
Intervals

Intervals are, you could view this as, a language for musicians. When speaking to another person about music, you both need to use consistent terminology. For example, if I went to a farming town deep into China and asked where the Great Wall was, he most likely would have no idea what I was saying. I would be asking a question that he could understand if we both spoke with words that had the same meaning.

How can we apply that to music? I always ask a student, "How many notes are on your guitar" and they look at me like it is some unimaginable number. I surprise them when I answer, 12. There are only twelve notes in Western music.

The notes that we use are thus:

> **Example 2-1:**
>
> ## A – A# – B – C – C# – D – D# – E – F – F# – G – G#

Then it starts back over at *A* (The solitary note "A" is confusing, so I will make it bold when I am talking about a note). Example 2-1 is commonly referred to as the chromatic scale.

You may notice that Ex. 2-1 has no flatted notes. This are referred to as enharmonic notes. What that means is there are two notes that look differently, but mean the same thing, e.g. *A#* and *Bb*. Then there is another way of looking at the twelve notes:

> **Example 2-2:**
>
> ## A – Bb – B – C – Db – D – Eb – E – F – Gb – G – Ab

Then it starts over again at *A*.

The # means sharp and the *b* means flat. When you move up, i.e. from the first fret to the second fret, you sharpen the pitch. When you move down, i.e. from the second fret to the first fret, you flatten the pitch. With this said, if you start on the 5th string (the second string from the top) or *A*-string open (not fretted) the pitch is an *A.* If you move up the guitar (linearly, on one string) every fret you move up will sharpen and it will correspond with Ex.2-1 and Ex.2-2 (see Diagram 2-1, notice that the pattern starts over at 12).

The notes *A B C D E F G* are called naturals. The in-between notes *A# C# D# F# G#* or enharmonically, *Bb Db Eb Gb Ab* are called accidentals. This is a good thing to memorize, or do a note-to-self on this idea (whenever you see <u>*NTS*</u> that means note to self, or it would be a good idea to remember this). These will be used for the rest of your life, if you don't give up music that is, and if you did, shame on you.

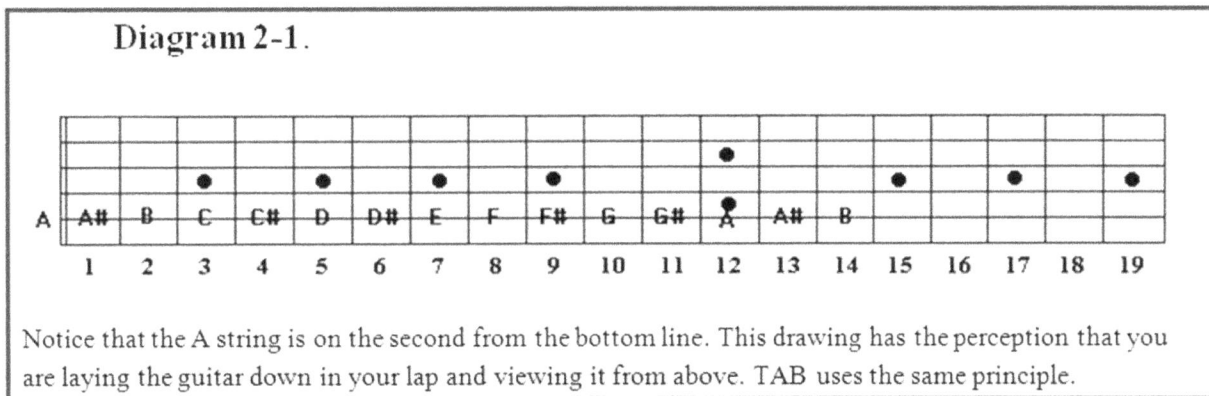

Diagram 2-1.

A	A#	B	C	C#	D	D#	E	F	F#	G	G#	A	A#	B					
	1	2	3	4	5	6	7	8	9	10	11	12	13	14	15	16	17	18	19

Notice that the A string is on the second from the bottom line. This drawing has the perception that you are laying the guitar down in your lap and viewing it from above. TAB uses the same principle.

These notes, when put into the context of a scale, are called intervals. The next chapter will begin scale theory. This will be covered again in the major scale chapter, as well. Let's say we have the *C major* scale *C-D-E-F-G-A-B-C.* The first note in the scale (*C*) is the first interval; the second note (*D*) is the second interval. That's pretty easy, isn't it? When talking to another person about music you may say, "The progression is I-IV-V (1-4-5)", or you may say, "The harmonic minor is the same as the natural minor, but with a raised 7th". These explanations involve intervals that relate to a scale.

In Western music, scales have 7 notes, thus 7 intervals. We characterize them by either uppercase or lowercase Roman (UCR or LCR) numerals. The most common progression (which will be explained later) is:

Example 2-3:

I – ii – iii – IV – V – vi – vii

As you can see in Example 2-3, the 1, 4, and 5 are UCR numerals and the 2, 3, 6, and 7 are LCR. *(NTS)*

We now know that there are 7 intervals in Western music. These can be categorized as such: Major (M), Minor (m), Perfect (P), Augmented (A), and Diminished (d).

When you play notes one after the other, it is called a melodic interval. Notes played at the same time it is called a harmonic interval. If you play a solo you build a melody, but if you play a chord the notes need to harmonize (sound good together) or it sounds like it is wrong (dissonance). So, if I said that I played a melody with a 1st and a 2nd, then it would be clear (using the *C major* scale example above) that I played a *C* then a *D*. If I said that I played a chord consisting of a 1st and a 2nd, then it would be clear that I played a *C* and *D* at the same time. This will be important later.

Regarding the interval categories, there can be various types of intervals, because as you can see from Example 2-1, there are twelve notes and from the *C major* scale above, there are only 7 (It looks like 8, but a *C* is a *C* is a *C*. These are the same note, so there is a 1st and an octave, which is usually referred to as a 1st since the scale just repeats itself). There are 5 notes not being played. If you substitute / interchange a note then you have altered the scale and thus, the interval. Let me give you an example. If you have the *A major* scale (*A-B-C#-D-E-F#-G#*) and you changed out the *B* for a B*b*, then it isn't an *A major* scale anymore because the Major 2nd has been changed to a minor 2nd.

Scale theory is later in the book. Come back if you need to go over the material again. The Major (M), Minor (m), Perfect (P), Augmented (A), and Diminished (d) are terms used to express certain intervals. Seconds, thirds, sixths, and sevenths can all be major (or minor) intervals, but fourths, fifths, and octaves are called perfect intervals, in both major and minor keys. If we put this in perspective to the intervals we have this:

Example 2-4:

Root, m2, M2, m3, M3, P4, A4, P5, A5, M6, m7, M7, and lastly the Octave.

The m2 is minor 2nd, the M2 is major 2nd, the P4 is perfect 4th, and the A4 is an augmented 4th. If we match Example 2-4 up with Example 2-1 it will paint a clearer picture (Ex 2-5).

Example 2-5:

A	A#	B	C	C#	D	D#	E	F	F#	G	G#	A
Root	m2	M2	m3	M3	P4	A4	P5	A5	M6	m7	M7	Octave

Remember, the *A* major scale is *A-B-C#-D-E-F#-G#, and* we inserted a *Bb* (*A #,* think enharmonic) in the place of a *B*. Notice that the interchanged note of B*b* (*A#* is the same thing,) for B takes the interval from a M2 to m2. You don't need to understand this fully, just the concept.

Just remember that an interval is the distance from the 1st note (also called the root or tonic) to the next note. So, the 2nd interval is the 2nd note in the scale, and it will correspond with either a m2 or a M2 depending on the distance between the 1st note and the 2nd. For example, say I am playing in the key of *A* major, the *A* is the 1st note and the next note I play is a *B*. The *B* is the 2nd interval in the scale. You can see in Example 2-5 that *B* is the M2 (Major 2nd) compared to the root (*A*).

Using this terminology one could say that they were playing off of the 3rd of the chord. This would mean that they would be playing a scale as it relates to the chord in general, but more specifically how it relates to the 3rd note in the chord. One could also say that they were playing a minor third in the place of where a major third of a scale is supposed to be played (consequently making a melodic minor, but that is later). This goes into chord theory which hasn't been discussed yet, but you get the idea that terminology is vital to know before you move on.

RECAP:

🎵 There are 12 notes in Western music.

🎵 Most scales only use 7 of the 12 notes.

🎵 These notes correspond to an interval. The first note is the 1st interval.

🎵 These intervals can be categorized into M, m, P, A, & d.

🎵 The abbreviated notation for intervals are uppercase or lowercase Roman (UCR or LCR) numerals.

This basis of theory will be developed further as we progress. Keep these ideas in mind. I will describe the notation better and its use in the preceding chapters. I will use the interval terminology from here on out. So, if you haven't got it down, look it over once more. Now, we go on to the Major scale.

Chapter 3
Major Scales

The major scale is the foundation of music. Knowing this and using your brain with this key of information will unlock a million doors. Good pitch, right? Well, it's true. Why is a minor scale, minor? Why is a chord a chord? And many more questions can be answered by understanding the major scale.

In order to first go through the concepts, we need to know about steps. Steps are what we take to get somewhere, just like when we walk. We put one step in front of the other. In music we do the same thing. If you look at your guitar, or Diagram 3-1, you see strings and frets. Ignore the various strings and concentrate on the top string.

If we go linearly (up the neck from the nut toward the bridge) we traverse over frets. If we go from the 1st fret to the 2nd fret we have gone a half step (1/2 step or just H). If we go from the 1st fret to the 3rd fret then we have traveled a whole step (1 step or just W). Now if we go from the 1st fret to the 4th fret we have just made a one and a half step (1 ½ step).

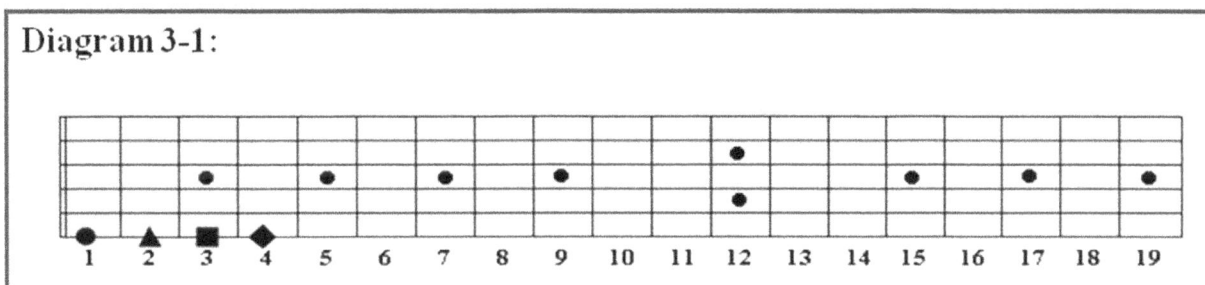

Diagram 3-1:

You can see in Diagram 3-1 that if you go from the circle to the triangle, ½ step. Go from the circle to the square, 1 step. Go from the circle to the diamond makes 1 ½ step. This is true from the open string as well. The open string to the 1st fret ½ step, to the 2nd fret 1 step, to the 3rd fret is 1 ½ step.

Note: There isn't a 2 step interval in Western music. One could bend a string to sound out to the pitch of 2 steps up, but a scale does not make a 2 step interval (Never say never, but 99.9% of the time).

The major scale is a diatonic scale. This term "diatonic" is used to refer mainly to "concerning the major scale" and sometimes in referring to any 7 note scale. It is used to mean the major scale and the modes from the major scale. So, when saying that I practiced diatonic harmony, it means that I used the major scale or a mode of the major scale to make music. This would exclude the melodic minor scale, the harmonic minor scale, the enigmatic scale, Hungarian minor, and many, many more.

Now we know what a step is, what an interval is, and what diatonic means. Now how do we make this thing? And what use is it to me? There is a formula that is used to make the major scale. This formula is:

Example 3-1:

W – W – H – W – W – W –H   (*NTS:* Know this!!!)

Recall that **W** means **whole step** and **H** means **half step**. We are going to use a keyboard from a piano to help us understand this.

Diagram 3-2:

Notice that I only have the naturals **C D E F G A B C** printed on the keyboard. This is because the foundation of music is the major scale, and the foundation of the major scale is the *C major* scale. The step progression illustrated in Example 3-1 is the outline by which we can get the *C major* scale. You can visualize this better if you view each key as a half step. The black keys are the accidentals that lie between certain naturals. Make note that there are 7 naturals and 5 accidentals. It is easier to see this on a piano than on a guitar fretboard.

When you go from *C* to *D* it is a whole step, *D* to *E* whole step, *E* to *F* half step, *F* to *G* whole step, *G* to *A* whole step, *A* to *B* whole step, and from *B* back to *C* is a half step.

Why isn't the foundation of the major scale *A major* instead of *C major*, and why that step progression? This is because the notes that are the outcome of the W–W–H–W–W–W–H have harmonic balance. That should be good enough of an explanation for now. The *C major* is used because there are no sharps (#) or flats (*b*) in this scale and we use that step progression because of the harmonic balance. Therefore we use it as the foundation. Now we need to play the major scale.

TAB 3-1 shows us the *C major* scale played with the root note (the root of C major is C) on the *A* string, in one octave. The first note and the last note are of the same quality (both are *C*) but the second C that is played is of a higher pitch. The term octave (written as *8va*) is Latin for 8. So, it is the 8th note in the scale and is also considered a 1st interval if the scale was to continue in this pattern, and it is of the same note quality as the 1st note. The octave of *C* cannot be *C#*, *D* or any other quality, but only *C*.

Notice that I didn't post a linear TAB of the major scale. That is because that not many people use scales in a linear fashion under most circumstances. It is good knowledge to know this though. The notes are the same enharmonically. That means that the notes are of the same pitch and note quality, but located on a different fret and string. TAB 3-2 is the C major scale on one string (linearly).

TAB 3-2:

If you fret out TAB 3-2, you will see that it carries the progression W–W–H–W–W–W–H.

THE CYCLE OF 5ths

The *C major* scale plays a part in all of the other major scales. We use a method known as the Cycle of 5ths. The Cycle of 5ths is exactly what it sounds like. We take the 5th interval of a major scale and that note becomes the 1st interval of the next major scale. Let me show you.

We first start with the C major scale, because it is the foundation of all major scales.

C – D – E – F – G – A – B – C

Then we go to the 5th interval (Remember that *C* is the 1st interval!! This is where many people make a mistake). This note is *G*, I'll show you:

C – D – E – F – G.

The **G** will now be the 1st interval of the next major scale.

G – A – B – C – D – E – F♯ – G

Wait a minute… did you remember the step progression?

W–W–H–W–W–W–H

The *C major* scale will be the **ONLY** major scale that is all naturals (**_NTS_**). All major scales will have at least one # or one *b* in them, except for the *C* major scale. These major scales are also referred to as keys. We will explain why in the chord chapter, but for now let's use the terminology.

The key of *C major* has produced the next key, *G major*. Let's keep going. We go to the 5th interval of the *G major* scale (notice key and scale are interchangeable when referring to their properties, but you play a *G major* scale not a *G major* key. You play *in* a *G major* key not a *G major* scale).

G – A – B – C – D

Now the new key is the key of *D major*.

D – E – F♯ – G – A – B – C♯ – D

Go to the 5th interval of D major.

D – E – F♯ – G – A

The new key is *A major*.

A – B – C♯ – D – E – F♯ – G♯ – A

This keeps on going until we reach the key of C#, so I'll just put up a diagram so you can see it as a whole.

Diagram 3-3:

$$C - D - E - F - G - A - B - C$$
$$G - A - B - C - D - E - F\# - G$$
$$D - E - F\# - G - A - B - C\# - D$$
$$A - B - C\# - D - E - F\# - G\# - A$$
$$E - F\# - G\# - A - B - C\# - D\# - E$$
$$B - C\# - D\# - E - F\# - G\# - A\# - B$$
$$F\# - G\# - A\# - B - C\# - D\# - E\# - F\#$$
$$C\# - D\# - E\# - F\# - G\# - A\# - B\# - C\#$$

You really need to get out a pen and paper and see if you can come up with the same thing that I have. Practicing by writing these down, using the same convention, is a great way to remember the concepts, which can be more important than just memorizing the keys.

Note that the *C maj* scale has no sharps, the *G maj* scale has 1 sharp, the *D maj* scale has 2 sharps, the *A maj* scale has 3 sharps, and so on and so forth. The next thing to note is that *G maj* has one sharp and it is the *F#*. *D maj* has 2 sharps and they are *F#* and *C#*. *A maj* has 3 sharps and they are *F#*, *C#*, and *G#*. Also the new sharp is always the 7th interval. Interesting, isn't it? **<u>NTS:</u>** As the cycle of 5ths progresses, the number of sharps increases.

When you get a sharp, you keep a sharp. This means when you get the *F#* the next key will have the *F#* and another sharp, the *C#*. The next key will be *F#*, *C#*, and another sharp, *G#*. Lastly, know that the new sharp will be the 7th interval.

Diagram 3-4:

Key	No. of #'s	New # added	Total #'s
C – D – E – F – G – A – B – C	0		None
G – A – B – C – D – E – F♯ – G	1	F♯	F♯
D – E – F♯ – G – A – B – C♯ – D	2	C♯	F♯ C♯
A – B – C♯ – D – E – F♯ – G♯ – A	3	G♯	F♯ C♯ G♯
E – F♯ – G♯ – A – B – C♯ – D♯ – E	4	D♯	F♯ C♯ G♯ D♯
B – C♯ – D♯ – E – F♯ – G♯ – A♯ – B	5	A♯	F♯ C♯ G♯ D♯ A♯
F♯ – G♯ – A♯ – B – C♯ – D♯ – E♯ – F♯	6	E♯	F♯ C♯ G♯ D♯ A♯ E♯
C♯ – D♯ – E♯ – F♯ – G♯ – A♯ – B♯ – C♯	7	B♯	F♯ C♯ G♯ D♯ A♯ E♯ B♯

Now, I will put up some TAB on how I play the major scale. I usually play scales where there are 3 notes per string (3NPS). This lets me use as many notes as possible before I change to the next string. Four notes per string is possible, but shifting positions or the distance between the first note and last note will be a minimum of a 6 fret span.

In TAB 3-3 you can see that I have tabbed out the 3NPS major scales. These will correspond with the sharp keys displayed, in order, from Diagram 3-4. The note values will be displayed above the tab number and below the notation marks. Some of the scales will end on the root note and some won't. The reason I did this is to point out that a scale doesn't have to end on the root, and if you have the extra notes, make use of them.

TAB 3-3:

A B C♯ D E F♯ G♯ A B C♯ D E F♯ G♯ A B C♯ D
T A B
5 7 8 5 7 8 6 7 8 6 7 8 7 9 10 7 8 10

E F♯ G♯ A B C♯ D♯ E F♯ G♯ A B C♯ D♯ E
T A B
7 9 11 7 9 11 8 9 11 9 10 12 9 11 12

B C♯ D♯ E F♯ G♯ A♯ B C♯ D♯ E F♯ G♯ A♯ B C♯ D♯ E
T A B
7 9 11 7 9 11 8 9 11 8 9 11 9 11 12 9 11 12

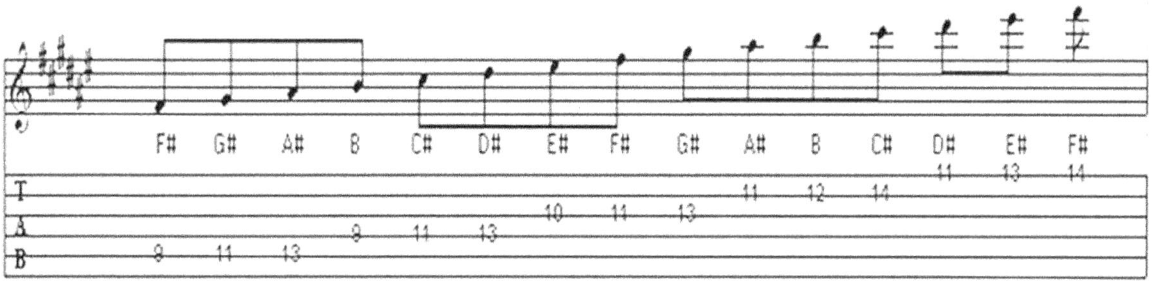
F♯ G♯ A♯ B C♯ D♯ E♯ F♯ G♯ A♯ B C♯ D♯ E♯ F♯
T A B
9 11 13 9 11 13 10 11 13 11 12 14 11 13 14

The notes above the tab read: C# D# E# F# G# A# B# C# D# E# F# G# A# B# C# D# E# F#

If you take a good, hard look at all of the scales, you will notice that they look very similar to each other in the way that you play them. The only difference is that they're on different frets and/or strings. Remember that the major scale is not the notes, per se, but the step progression. The step progression is how you derive the notes, so they should all look very much alike.

Here is an important thing to know about scales. There can only be one letter per interval. By that I mean, you cannot have an *A* and an *A#* in the same scale. You can, however, have an *A* and a *Bb*. It's just too confusing, that is why there are enharmonic notes. Another thing to note is that you need one "letter" of each. All major scales will have an A−B−C−D−E−F−G of some nature, be it a natural, sharp, or flat. The main reason I started the scales on these particular frets isn't because they are easier, but they are easier to remember. I use memorization tools a lot. Let me show you.

Take the first note from each of these major scales (keys) and put them on a fret board.

Diagram 3-5:

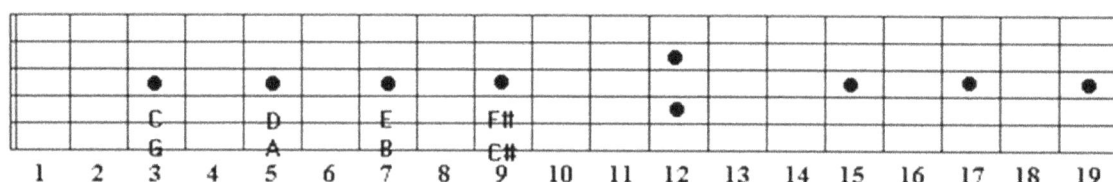

Look at the pattern:

C is on the 3rd fret. Right above that is the *G*. Move over 2 frets and down a string is the *D*. Then you go up a string to the *A*. And the pattern continues exactly like that until the *C#*. Remember that this is the Cycle of 5ths? Then obviously, a 5th on a guitar is when you move up a string or when you move over 2 frets and down a string. This would be a good thing to remember. There is an exception with the *B* string. You will grow to learn that one string usually makes you move over a fret toward the bridge.

Here's another memory device I use to help remember the sharps added. The first thing to remember is that the newly added sharp is the 7th interval. Most people want to count up to the 7, but it is way easier to move down. Think about it. The 1st interval is also the 8th, then one half step backwards (in a major scale) is the 7th interval. So, what is the sharp in *G*? The *F#*! Which is one half step behind the *G* note. Let me give you an illustration.

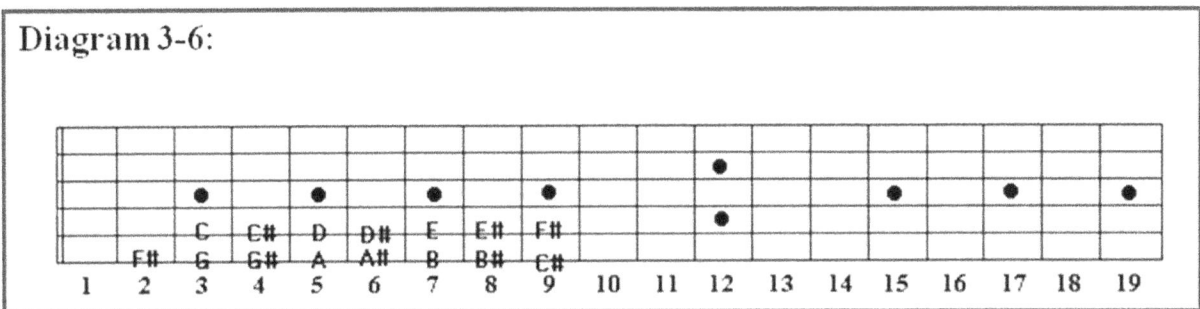

Diagram 3-6:

You can easily see by comparing the Diagrams 3-5 and 3-6 that the new sharps are added much in the same manner that the new sharp keys are added, in 5ths. Here's a diagram without the sharp keys in it.

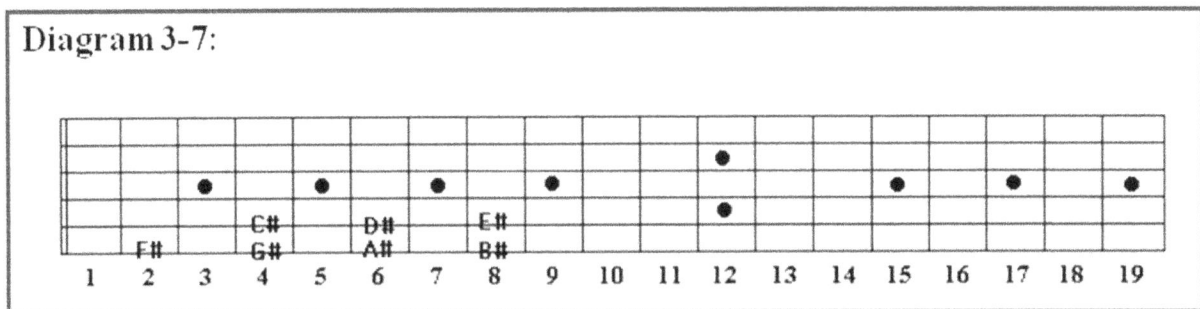

Diagram 3-7:

Now you can see the pattern of sharps. For a memory tool, I say *C* has no sharps, *G* has one sharp an *F#*, *D* has two sharps, a *F#* and a *C#*, *A* has three sharps, a *F#*, a *C#*, and a *G#*, and so on. If you go through this method, you can see how this diagram correlates exactly with Diagram 3-4.

THE CYCLE OF 4ths

This is very important to know!! Knowing your sharp keys is essential for guitar playing! There are 7 more keys though. These are the flat keys. Guitarists usually don't play in flat keys. These keys are normally used by pianists. If you play with a pianist, you better get to know flat keys. Some keys are easier to play on certain instruments because of their tuning and/or fingerings.

So we need to know flat keys. The main ones to store in the memory bank are the keys of *F* and *Bb*. These are the first two flat keys. I will explain all of the keys like before, but only tab out those 2 keys. This time though, we will use the Cycle of 4ths to create the next key (scale).

Again note: The *C major* scale will be the **ONLY** major scale that is all naturals (you should have done a **_NTS_** on this!!). All major scales will have at least one # or one *b* in them, except for the C major scale. These major scales are also referred to as keys.

The Cycle of 4ths is done exactly like the Cycle of 5ths, but with 4ths. We take the 4th interval of a major scale and that note becomes the 1st interval of the next major scale. Let me show you.

We first start with the C major scale, because it is the foundation of all major scales.

C – D – E – F – G – A – B – C

Then we go to the 4th interval (Remember that *C* is the 1st interval!!). This note is F:

C – D – E – F

The *F* will now be the 1st interval of the next major scale.

F – G – A – Bb – C – D – E – F

The key of *C major* has produced the next key, *F major*. We go to the 4th interval of the *F major* scale.

F – G – A – Bb

Now the new key is the key of *Bb major*.

Bb – C – D – Eb – F – G – A – Bb

Go to the 4th interval of Bb major.

Bb – C – D – Eb

The new key is *Eb major*.

Eb – F – G – Ab – Bb – C – D – Eb

This keeps on going until we reach the key of *Cb*. Here's diagram so you can see it as a whole.

```
Diagram 3-8:
C – D – E – F – G – A – B – C
F – G – A – Bb – C – D – E – F
Bb – C – D – Eb – F – G – A – Bb
Eb – F – G – Ab – Bb – C – D – Eb
Ab – Bb – C – Db – Eb – F – G – Ab
Db – Eb – F – Gb – Ab – Bb – C – Db
Gb – Ab – Bb – Cb – Db – Eb – F – Gb
Cb – Db – Eb – Fb – Gb – Ab – Bb – Cb
```

Again, you really need to get out a pen and paper and see if you can come up with the same thing outcome.

Note that the *C maj* scale has no flats, the *F maj* scale has 1 flat, the *Bb maj* scale has 2 flats, the *Eb maj* scale has 3 flats, and so on. The next thing to note is that *F maj* has one flat and it is the *Bb*. *Bb maj* has 2 flats and they are *Bb* and *Eb*. *Eb maj* has 3 flats and they are *Bb*, *Eb*, and *Ab*. Also, the new flat is always the 4th interval.

NTS: As the cycle of 4ths progresses, the number of flats increases. When you get a flat, you keep a flat. Just like with the sharps. This means when you get the *Bb* the next key will have the *Bb*. In fact the next key will be the *Bb* and another flat. The new flat always becomes the next new key. This is much easier to learn than the 5ths. The next key will be *Bb*, *Eb*, and another flat, *Ab* (see Diagram 3-9).

Diagram 3-9:

Key	No. of b's	New b added	Total b's
C – D – E – F – G – A – B – C	0		None
F – G – A – Bb – C – D – E – F	1	Bb	Bb
Bb – C – D – Eb – F – G – A – Bb	2	Eb	Bb Eb
Eb – F – G – Ab – Bb – C – D – Eb	3	Ab	Bb Eb Ab
Ab – Bb – C – Db – Eb – F – G – Ab	4	Db	Bb Eb Ab Db
Db – Eb – F – Gb – Ab – Bb – C – Db	5	Gb	Bb Eb Ab Db Gb
Gb – Ab – Bb – Cb – Db – Eb – F – Gb	6	Cb	Bb Eb Ab Db Gb Cb
Cb – Db – Eb – Fb – Gb – Ab – Bb – Cb	7	Fb	Bb Eb Ab Db Gb Cb

If you take the time to look at both Diagrams 3-4 and 3-9 beside each other you will see that they are upside down from each other. Here they are in order:

Diagram 3-10:

Sharp Key	Flat Key
C – D – E – F – G – A – B – C	C – D – E – F – G – A – B – C
G – A – B – C – D – E – F# – G	F – G – A – Bb – C – D – E – F
D – E – F# – G – A – B – C# – D	Bb – C – D – Eb – F – G – A – Bb
A – B – C# – D – E – F# – G# – A	Eb – F – G – Ab – Bb – C – D – Eb
E – F# – G# – A – B – C# – D# – E	Ab – Bb – C – Db – Eb – F – G – Ab
B – C# – D# – E – F# – G# – A# – B	Db – Eb – F – Gb – Ab – Bb – C – Db
F# – G# – A# – B – C# – D# – E# – F#	Gb – Ab – Bb – Cb – Db – Eb – F – Gb
C# – D# – E# – F# – G# – A# – B# – C#	Cb – Db – Eb – Fb – Gb – Ab – Bb – Cb

Now I will invert (flip) the flat keys upside down.

Sharp Key	Flat Key
C – D – E – F – G – A – B – C	Cb – Db – Eb – Fb – Gb – Ab – Bb – Cb
G – A – B – C – D – E – F♯ – G	Gb – Ab – Bb – Cb – Db – Eb – F – Gb
D – E – F♯ – G – A – B – C♯ – D	Db – Eb – F – Gb – Ab – Bb – C – Db
A – B – C♯ – D – E – F♯ – G♯ – A	Ab – Bb – C – Db – Eb – F – G – Ab
E – F♯ – G♯ – A – B – C♯ – D♯ – E	Eb – F – G – Ab – Bb – C – D – Eb
B – C♯ – D♯ – E – F♯ – G♯ – A♯ – B	Bb – C – D – Eb – F – G – A – Bb
F♯ – G♯ – A♯ – B – C♯ – D♯ – E♯ – F♯	F – G – A – Bb – C – D – E – F
C♯ – D♯ – E♯ – F♯ – G♯ – A♯ – B♯ – C♯	C – D – E – F – G – A – B – C

The notes correlate to each other now. Well, you don't need to know that, but it does help you to remember things and put them into perspective.

Here are the F and Bb major scales tabbed out:

TAB 3-4:

This brings us to a new idea involving these major scales. Remember I was talking about keys? If you take a look at the far left side of the tabs posted so far, you can see a number of sharps and flats beside the 𝄞. This is the key signature.

If there is one *b* then you know that the following music is in the key of *F*, because the *F* major scale only has 1 flat. If you see 2 #'s then you know that the following music is in the key of *D*, because the *D* major scale has only 2 sharps. If we see no sharps or flats then we know that the following music is in the key of *C*, because the *C* major scale has neither sharps nor flats. And of course this goes for all keys with sharps and flats.

Knowing the major keys (scales) will be very useful in the next chapter. Take the time to write out the major scales. Figure out how many sharps or flats are in the major scales. Lock this into memory. Some people use Mnemonics like:

Get **D**ave **A**n **E**xtra **B**ass **F**or **C**hristmas

Fred **B**etter **E**at **A**nother **D**ozen **G**reasy **C**orndogs

This works for some people. It may do you some good to try to come up with ones of your own also.

Think about it… If you know what key someone is playing in, then if you want to play a guitar solo over that key, you just play the scale that the key is in. Playing the key of C major? Play the C major scale over it. Playing in the key of G major? Play the G major scale over it. That should be easy enough to understand. We will get into more detail of soloing later after more theory is covered.

Chapter 4
Chord Theory

Here is where the scale theory is going to come into practice. If you don't have that down, this may get a little complicated. Chord theory in itself is not complicated, but like any form of education, things build incrementally. The chords are built out of the major scales and are bound by rules.

Triads are the foundation of a chord. One rule to note is that a chord must have 3 notes in order to be considered a chord. In rock music people use "power chords" these are 2 note chords. Although people use these power chords a lot, but as you will see, they are not a legitimate chord.

Triads are made of 3 notes. We need to understand that 3 notes means 3 different notes. Many people forget that if we play a *C* and on another string we play a "different" *C*, this constitutes two notes. This is wrong. A *C* is a *C* is a *C*. You recall me saying that in the major scale chapter? The same goes for chords.

We will use a method to build these triads. In order to do so, you have to know some terminology. There are 4 types of triads:

♫ *Major* triads

♫ *minor* triads

♫ *diminished* triads

♫ *augmented* triads

We have already seen these words from the interval chapter. Now we will discuss the terminology.

Triads are built by stacking thirds. These thirds come from major scales. We will call these scales keys. These keys are the guidelines. When we play in a key, the idea is to forget all the notes that are not in the key. So, focus only on the notes in the key. Let's use *C* major because it is the easiest to work with because it has no #'s or *b*'s.

C – D – E – F – G – A – B – C

As you can see there is no *C#, D#, F#, G#,* or *A#*. While we work with this key, put them in the corner of your mind, for now. We start with the first note *C* and then we build on it.

C – keep this and count up 3 notes (Remember *C* is 1) and get the note *E*. So, *E* is the next note. Since a triad has 3 notes, we count up 3 more notes from *E* (*E* is now 1) and we get *G*. We put these together and that's a triad (*CEG*). Yes, it's just that easy. But here is where the knowledge comes in.

There are major and minor thirds. These are being used when stacking the thirds, it's just not obvious. We need to go to all 12 notes to see it though. First, let me explain what a major and minor third is. For all further notations, I will use the moniker 3 or 3rd for a major third and b3 for a minor third. Remember, W means whole step and H means half step.

A major third is made by adding two whole steps (W-W).

A minor third is made by adding either a W and a H or by adding a H and a W. W-H and H-W add up to the same thing. Let's view this by using all 12 notes, starting on *C*.

> **Example 4-1:**
>
> C – C# – D – D# – E – F – F# – G – G# – A – A# – B – C

Taking the *C* and using it as the first note of the triad, we take two whole steps and end up on *E*. From *E* we take a half step and a whole step and end up on *G*. This is what we get:

C + W-W = *E*

E + H-W = *G*

Put these together and we get *CEG*.

The major third plus a minor third formula is how a **major chord** is made.

Why did we use a H-W for the minor third and not W-H?

Look at the *C* major scale:

C – D – E – F – G – A – B – C

There is no *F#*, right? If we went from *E* and then went W-H it would have gone to *F#* then to *G* and this isn't how the *C* major scale is written. We have to use all of the notes and use the key interchangeably. You have to see the key and see in between the notes. Just because they aren't written down doesn't mean they don't exist. They are just being passed over.

So, my first example of stacking thirds was much easier than this example. It's like using a calculator. You punch in the numbers and hit equal. The calculator does the work and you see the result. Using the key and stacking thirds does the work of the major and minor third stacking, but without all of the work. The key has done that for you. Remember, the step progression of a major scale:

W – W – H – W – W – W –H

W-W + H-W is a major chord, see it? Ok, what is a minor chord then? Maybe you have guessed it already, but if not, a minor chord is a b3 + 3. Therefore, we have W-H (or H-W) + W-W.

If we used the 12 notes in Example 4-1, we see that this correlates to the notes:

C-Eb-G

See the *Eb*? Compared to the C major chord the 3rd interval has been flattened from *E* to *Eb*. A **minor chord** is defined as such. All other notes (besides the 1st) can be altered and not the 3rd and it <u>won't</u> be minor. The 3rd note can be flattened and all other notes remain the same and it <u>is</u> minor. The interval of the 3rd is the reason a chord is major or minor (***NTS***). Do you remember M3 and m3 intervals? If not, see Example 4-3.

When creating a chord we use 3 notes by stacking thirds. These notes equate to the 1st note (root) of the major scale, 3rd note (3rd interval) of the major scale, and 5th note (5th interval) of the major scale. The root note is used to build the chord. The 3rd is produced from the 1st interval, and the 5th is produced from the 3rd interval.

C – D – E – F – G – A – B – C

Example 4-2:

C	D	E	F	G	A	B	C
1st interval Or Root	2nd interval	3rd interval	4th interval	5th interval	6th interval	7th interval	Octave(8va)

Let's correlate this table to another table from the interval chapter.

Example 4-3:

C	C#/	D	D#/E	E	F	F#/G	G	G#/	A	A#/	B	C
Root	m2	M	m3	M	P	A4	P5	A5	M6	m7	M7	Octave

Notice when we made the *C* minor chord we don't use *D#* because there is a *D* in the key of *C*. When we refer to a chord, we refer it back to its **own major scale**. If we talk about a *D* chord, we don't say it is major because of the *C* major scale (because in fact it would be minor compared to the C major scale). We say it is major because it has a major 3rd as compared to the <u>D major</u> scale. We say a *B* minor is minor because it has a minor third as compared to the <u>B major</u> scale.

Quick Recap So Far:

🎵 Triads are the 1-3-5 of a chord that are produced by stacking thirds

🎵 Major third = W-W

🎵 Minor third = H-W or W-H

🎵 Major chord = 3 + b3

🎵 Minor chord = *b3* + 3

If we play a song, and the song is in a key, then why are there many chords being played? There are 7 base chords (triads) in a key. These chords relate to the 7 notes in the scale (intervals). Each note has its own triad/chord. We will lock our self in to a key, let's make it *C* major. And we will build all seven chords possible from this key. The "1st chord" is the chord that is built from the first interval (root) of the major scale. The "2nd chord" is the chord that is built from the second note of the same major scale that the 1st chord was built from. And so on.

Table 4-1:

Chord	1st note	3rd note	5th note	1-3-5	Type of
1st	C	E	G	C-E-G	Major
2nd	D	F	A	D-F-A	minor
3rd	E	G	B	E-G-B	minor
4th	F	A	C	F-A-C	Major
5th	G	B	D	G-B-D	Major
6th	A	C	E	A-C-E	minor
7th	B	D	F	B-D-F	diminished

This is how it was constructed:

Use 1-3-5 from the *C* major scale.

C – D – E – F – G – A – B – C

And get *C-E-G*

Then go to the next interval (*D*) and took the 1-3-5.

D – E – F – G – A – B – C – D

And get *D-F-A*

Then go to the next interval (*E*) and found the 1-3-5.

E – F – G – A – B – C – D – E

And get *E-G-B*

Then continue all of the way through, as you can see by Table 4-1.

The chords produced are major or minor based on referring the notes back to their <u>own</u> major scales. Table 4-2 has the major scales for these seven intervals. Read Table 4-2 from left to right.

Table 4-2:

C maj	C	D	E	F	G	A	B	C
D maj	D	E	F#	G	A	B	C#	D
E maj	E	F#	G#	A	B	C#	D#	E
F maj	F	G	A	Bb	C	D	E	F
G maj	G	A	B	C	D	E	F#	G
A maj	A	B	C#	D	E	F#	G#	A
B maj	B	C#	D#	E	F#	G#	A#	B

When comparing the 1st, 3rd, and 5th intervals to their own major scales we see:

Table 4-3:

1-3-5	Compared to own maj scale	Type of chord
C-E-G	1-3-5	Major
D-F-A	1-b3-5	minor
E-G-B	1-b3-5	minor
F-A-C	1-3-5	Major
G-B-D	1-3-5	Major
A-C-E	1-b3-5	minor
B-D-F	1-b3-b5	diminished

🎵 The 3rd of *D*, from the *D* major scale, is *F#* not *F*. *F* is down ½ step from *F#* meaning that it has been flattened. So, the 3rd is flat making it a minor chord.

🎵 The 3rd of *E*, from the *E* major scale, is *G#* not *G*. *G* is down ½ step from *G#* meaning that it has been flattened. So, the 3rd is flat making it a minor chord.

🎵 The 3rd of *A*, from the *A* major scale, is *C#* not *C*. *C* is down ½ step from *C#* meaning that it has been flattened. So, the 3rd is flat making it a minor chord.

🎵 The 3rd of *B*, from the *B* major scale, is *D#* not *D*. *D* is down ½ step from *D#* meaning that it has been flattened. So, the 3rd is flat making it a minor chord. Also, the 5th is an *F#* in the *B* major scale not an *F*, therefore the 5th has been flattened as well. This brings up another type of chord, the diminished. A diminished chord is made by stacking two minor thirds (there is a little more about diminished that will be explained in the 7th chords chapter).

We see that the order of the chord types in a major scale is:

Example 4-4 (Chord Mantra):

M-m-m-M-M-m-d (*NTS*)

M = major, m = minor, and d = diminished.

All major scales follow this order. Every 2nd chord (a chord that is made from the 2nd interval) is minor, every 3rd is minor, 4th is major, etc.

It would do you a great service to memorize that order.

🎵 Ok then, what is the 3rd chord in the key of *A*?

Look to the *A* major scale and see that the 3rd interval is *C#* (Table 4-2). From memory (and the example above) we know that the 3rd chord is always a minor chord. Therefore we know that the 3rd chord in the key of *A* is *C#* minor.

Here is the reason that we use the uppercase Roman (UCR) and lowercase Roman (LCR) numbers as described in the intervals chapter.

The UCR numerals are designated for a **major** chord. The LCR numerals are designated for a **minor** chord. If you can't remember, UCR numerals are I-II-III-IV-V-VI-VII. The LCR numeration is i-ii-iii-iv-v-vi-vii. Easy enough, the UCR numerals are capital and the LCR are lowercase. This is the order of the chords in every major scale.

> **Example 4-5:**
>
> **I – ii – iii – IV – V – vi – vii**
>
> I – IV – V = major
>
> ii – iii – vi = minor
>
> vii = diminished

A diminished has a *b*3. That means that theoretically it is a minor chord. That is why the LCR number is used for the diminished. Just know that the 7th interval of any major scale always produces a diminished chord.

By using the Example 4-5 we can see that the chords are referenced by these UCR or LCR numerals, not notes or intervals. If we have a chord progression that uses the 1st, 4th, and 5th chord from a key, we say it is the I, IV, and V chord. The UCR numeration means a major chord.

If we are in the key of *C* major and we use the I-IV-V terminology, we should automatically think of the *C* major chord, *F* major chord, and *G* major chord, in that order. Now if I said IV-V-I, it would imply the *F* major chord, *G* major chord, and *C* major chord.

I could use LCR numbers for what is usually a UCR numeral. If I used a chord progression of I-iv-V, the 4th chord is a minor chord. This means that the 4th

chord has been changed from what it should be, in regard to the major scale that is being referenced.

For example, if we are in the key of *C* major and we use the previous chord progression of I-iv-V the chords will be *C* major, *F* <u>minor</u>, and *G* major. The UCR or LCR symbols indicate specifically major or minor.

Now if I had a chord progression that was ii-vii-I, we can see that we are using the diminished chord. Remember that the vii is diminished. It uses LCR numeration because the 3rd in the chord is flattened, but recall that the 5th is also flattened, making it diminished. So the chord progression in the key of *C* major for ii-vii-I is *D* minor, *B* diminished, and *C* major.

Work these out by writing out a major scale and then make up progressions like I-IV-V or I-vi-ii-V, or whatever, in any order. See if you can figure out the progression and then play it and see what it sounds like.

Here is an easy reference chart for the chords in every key:

Table 4-4:

Key	I	ii	iii	IV	V	vi	Vii
C	C	D	E	F	G	A	B
G	G	A	B	C	D	E	F#
D	D	E	F#	G	A	B	C#
A	A	B	C#	D	E	F#	G#
E	E	F#	G#	A	B	C#	D#
B	B	C#	D#	E	F#	G#	A#
F#	F#	G#	A#	B	C#	D#	E#
C#	C#	D#	E#	F#	G#	A#	B#
F	F	G	A	Bb	C	D	E
Bb	Bb	C	D	Eb	G	A	B
Eb	Eb	F	G	Ab	Bb	C	D
Ab	Ab	Bb	C	Db	Eb	F	G
Dd	Db	Eb	F	Gb	Ab	Bb	C
Gb	Gb	Ab	Bb	Cb	Db	Eb	F
Cb	Cb	Db	Eb	Fb	Gb	Ab	Bb

As I have stated before a triad (the basis of a chord) is 1-3-5. This doesn't mean that it has to be played in that order. Inversions are triads that move the 1-3-5 into a different arrangement. 5-1-3 is still using the same 3 notes, but in a different order. Table 4-5 shows the 2 different triad inversions.

Table 4-5:

Inversion	Order of notes	Example in C major	Example in A minor
Normal triad no inversion	1-3-5	C-E-G	A-C-E
1st	3-5-1	E-G-C	C-E-A
2nd	5-1-3	G-C-E	E-A-C

There can be a third inversion, but this would require another note. So, obviously this wouldn't make it a triad. This concept of a third inversion will be discussed later.

People can make this very complicated. It really isn't that complicated. Terminology is the big issue. We speak about one note's relation to another note (interval) by numbers: 1st, 2nd, 3rd, etc. We speak about the notes in a scale by numbers: 1st note, 2nd note, 3rd note, etc. (some call the individual notes a degree of the scale: 1st degree, 2nd degree, 3rd degree, etc). We call the notes, as compared to the intervals in a scale, by numbers: 1st or root, minor 2nd, major 3rd, perfect 5th, etc. We speak of the makeup of a chord by numbers: "That chord is made up of a 1, 3, and 5, in C major. We talk about the chords in a progression by numbers: I-IV-V or 1-4-5, I-vi-ii-V or 1-6-2-5, etc. We even speak of the inversions by numbers: 1st inversion or 2nd inversion.

This may be confusing, but just look at the context of the discussion. Know your major scales and intervals. With the use of major scales, chord construction, and intervals all of the discussions can be understood. Saying, "in the key of C major, I'm playing I-IV-V." is much easier than saying, "In the key of C major, I'm playing a C major chord first, then a F major chord, and finally I am playing a G major chord. And then we start over and play the same three chords in a loop".

That is a long drawn out process and the terminology from the first sentence is much easier and means exactly the same thing.

Don't overcomplicate the concepts. Many people glance through a section, don't understand it, and move on. As if the next section that uses the ideas from the previous section is going to make more sense. Stay in a section of this book and use your pen and paper. Write out the 12 chromatic notes, **A − A# − B − C − C# − D − D# − E − F − F# − G − G#**, where the first note is in the key you are looking at working with. Build the major scale from the pattern **W-W-H-W-W-W-H.**

Once you have your major scale (in the key of *A* because I started the chromatic notes on *A*) **A-B-C#-D-E-F#-G#-A,** make all of your chords using the 1-3-5 concept: **A-C#-E, B-D-F#, C#-E-G#, D-F#-A, E-G#-B, F#-A-C#, G#-B-D**. After you have completed that, we know by **M-m-m-M-M-m-d** which chords are major, minor, or diminished, but confirm that idea by using the chords you made and comparing them to the chromatic scale that you wrote. Do the chords have the right patterns that make a major, minor, or diminished scale? If someone is playing a progression, ask what chords they are playing and try to figure out the key it's in.

That's how you learn theory, not reading this book. Use the knowledge. Incorporate the information. If you don't practice these concepts and ingrain them into your thinking, the theory will elude you. I spent many years without this knowledge. I sat down, wrote it out, and it all made sense.

From the theory that has been shown up till now, you should be able to understand:

♪ What a major scale is.

♪ The step progression that makes up a major scale.

♪ By what intervals a major scale is produced and what intervals are not in the major scale.

♪ The sharp keys that are created by the Cycle of 5ths.

♪ The flat keys that are created by the Cycle of 4ths.

♪ How many sharps or flats are in a certain key.

♪ The chords that are in specific keys.

♪ Whether these chords from specific keys are major, minor, or diminished.

♪ What makes a chord major, minor, or diminished.

♪ What the numerals of a chord progression mean.

♪ What an inversion is.

♪ Playing a scale over a chord progression.

Chapter 5
Seventh Chord Theory

We now understand major scale and chord theory that is based off of the major scale. We know how to make 1-3-5 triads, and their inversions. Now we need to add to or take away from the base chord to make seventh, extended, altered, and suspended chords.

Seventh chords are chords that use the 1-3-5 triad, which stack another third on top of that base triad. As you have guessed it looks like 1-3-5-7. I am using the numbers 1-3-5 and 1-3-5-7 loosely, because we now know that some notes are flat, as well as, sharp compared to their major scale. The notes could be 1-*b*3-5 or 1-*b*3-5-*b*7. It just depends on the chord and the scale degree.

Let's work out of *C* major to keep things easy and consistent. We still need the chromatic scale and we will need the key to understand this, along with the interval chart, and the chords built from the major scale.

Example 5-1:

$$C - C\# - D - D\# - E - F - F\# - G - G\# - A - A - \# - B - C$$

Example 5-2:

C	D	E	F	G	A	B	C
1st interval Or Root	*2nd interval*	*3rd interval*	*4th interval*	*5th interval*	*6th interval*	*7th interval*	*Octave(8va)*

Example 5-3:

C	C#/Db	D	D#/Eb	E	F	F#/Gb	G	G#/Ab	A	A#/Bb	B	C
Root	m2	M2	m3	M3	P4	A4	P5	A5	M6	m7	M7	Octave

Table 5-1:

Chord	1st note	3rd note	5th note	1-3-5	Type of chord
1st	C	E	G	C-E-G	Major
2nd	D	F	A	D-F-A	minor
3rd	E	G	B	E-G-B	minor
4th	F	A	C	F-A-C	Major
5th	G	B	D	G-B-D	Major
6th	A	C	E	A-C-E	minor
7th	B	D	F	B-D-F	diminished

I guess it is becoming apparent that learning this in order is necessary. These theories use preceding theories. So before we get started, if you need a recap, brush over the last couple chapters before beginning.

You should know by now the chords that are built from the major scale and whether they are major, minor, or diminished. These are going to be our building blocks. With these chords we will stack another third on them to make seventh chords. These sevenths chords come in many forms. This will make sense as we go through the chapter.

Example 5-4:

Major third = W+W

Minor third = W+H or H+W

Major triad = major third + minor third

Minor triad = minor third + major third

Diminished triad = minor third + minor third

Augmented triad = major third + major third

First, build the most basic seventh chord, the **major seventh chord**. This is usually written as a M7 chord, i.e. *C*M7, *D*M7, *Bb*M7, etc. It can also be written as *C*maj7, or *C*Δ. We will use the *C*M7 version. Build this by adding a major third to the major triad.

We know the major triad for *C* major is 1-3-5. Now stack a <u>major third</u> on top. The *C* chromatic scale below has the 1-3-5 indicated by being bold and of a larger font.

C – C# – D – D# – **E** – F – F# – **G** – G# – A – A# – B – C

Now add another major third, which is two whole steps. This indicates that the new note will be a *B*. So the CM7 chord will be 1-3-5-7 and the notes are indicated below on the *C* chromatic scale.

C – C# – D – D# – **E** – F – F# – **G** – G# – A – A# – **B** – C

Do you see the stacked thirds? They should be W-W then H-W and lastly, W-W. This makes a M7 chord.

The major chord doesn't always have a major seventh stacked on it. It could be what is termed a **dominant 7 chord**. Some people refer to this as a "7 chord" and it is written like this *C*7, *D*7, *Eb*7, etc. We take the major triad 1-3-5 just like before, but this time we stack a <u>minor third</u> on top.

C – C# – D – D# – **E** – F – F# – **G** – G# – A – **A#** – B – C

Of course since we already have an *A* as the 6th note of the scale we need to use the enharmonic term Bb for the minor seventh note. This C7 chord is built by the method 1-3-5-*b*7. This indicates that the 7th note is flattened <u>from its own major scale</u> not from the referenced scale.

Let me explain the last paragraph better. First thing to note, there is <u>only one dominant 7 chord</u> in a major key. This is <u>the 5th chord</u>. Let's view this better. To do this, I need to bring down the tables at the front of this chapter.

C	D	E	F	G	A	B	C
1st interval Or Root	2nd interval	3rd interval	4th interval	5th interval	6th interval	7th interval	Octave(8va)

C	C#/ Db	D	D#/ Eb	E	F	F#/ Gb	G	G#/ Ab	A	A#/ Bb	B	C
Root	m2	M2	m3	M3	P4	A4	P5	A5	M6	m7	M7	Octave

Chord	1st note	3rd note	5th note	1-3-5	Type of chord
1st	C	E	G	C-E-G	Major
2nd	D	F	A	D-F-A	minor
3rd	E	G	B	E-G-B	minor
4th	F	A	C	F-A-C	Major
5th	G	B	D	G-B-D	Major
6th	A	C	E	A-C-E	minor
7th	B	D	F	B-D-F	diminished

We can now see the *C* major scale, the intervals, and the chords made from the *C* major scale. The 5th chord in *C* major is a *G* major, but now we need to write the scale in the key of *C* major starting on the 5th note, *G*.

Example 5-5:

$$G - A - B - C - D - E - F - G$$

As we can see from Example 5-5 there are no sharps or flats. This indicates that the key is *C* major. Recall, only one key has no sharps or flats, *C* major. Only one key has one sharp and that is *G* major. *G* major has F # in the key of G major, not an *F*. All I have done is taken the C major scale and started it from a different point. If you don't understand this concept look back at the chord theory chapter and do some reviewing.

Referencing the G major scale we see that G major is **G-A-B-C-D-E-F#-G**. If we use the **1-3-5-7 shortcut**, we end up with *G-B-D-F#* and this isn't what we have in the key of *C*. We have *G-B-D-F*. I say shortcut because, do you recall the illustration I made to the calculator? The key has done the work of the W-W-H-W-W-W-H. When we apply the 1-3-5-7 to these major scales the major or minor thirds are being taken care of in the background. That's why we have to refer back to the note of topic's own major scale, and look at the interval chart. So, if we insert the G chromatic scale into our interval chart we get:

G	G#	A	A#	B	C	C#	D	D#	E	F	F#	G
Root	m2	M2	m3	M3	P4	A4	P5	A5	M6	m7	M7	Octave

Look at the *F#*. Do you see that *F#* correlates to a M7, but the *F* correlated to the m7? We have just proven that the 5th chord in *C* major, as a seventh chord, is *G7*. This is a dominant seventh chord. The 5th interval is the only dominant seventh chord in the major key.

The dominant seven has a specific character in chord progression charts. It is a superscript "7" over the right-hand side of the UCR numeral. Here are some examples I^7, II^7, V^7, etc. Based on the major scale the 5th chord is the only Dom7 chord. Therefore, you will usually only see the V^7 chord in most applications.

The next form of seventh chord is the **minor seventh** chord. The minor seventh chord is usually written as min7, m7, or -7, for example, *C*min7, *F*m7, or *A*-7. The m7 chord is a minor chord, 1-*b*3-5, with a minor third stacked on it. This makes 1-*b*3-5-*b*7. We will use the 2nd chord in C major to prove this. First we write out the C major scale starting on the 2nd note, D.

Example 5-6:

$$D - E - F - G - A - B - C - D$$

When we apply the 1-3-5-7 to this we get *D-F-A-C*. If we reference these notes to the *D* major scale (*D-E-F#-G-A-B-C#*) we see that *D* major has F # and a C#, not *F* and *C*. Then we know that we flatten the note when we move down from *F#* to *F* , as well as, when we go from *C#* to *C*. Lets visualize this with the interval chart.

D	D#	E	F	F#	G	G#	A	A#	B	C	C#	D
Root	m2	M2	m3	M3	P4	A4	P5	A5	M6	m7	M7	Octave

We start on *D* because we are talking about the *D*m7 chord, and we use the *D* major scale for the same reasons as before. The *D*m7 chord is *D-F-A-C*. The *F* and the *C* are flattened from the *D* major scale. We look at the interval chart with the *D* chromatic scale plugged in, and see that the *F* is a m3 and the *C* is a m7. We just proved that the seventh chord in the key of *C* major is a *D*m7.

The major scale has 7 chords in it: two are M7 chords, one is a dominant 7 chord, and three are m7 chords. That adds up to six, which means we still need to talk about that crazy diminished chord. The diminished takes some explaining.

The diminished chord has two different seventh chords. Let's review the first. The **diminished seventh chord** is commonly denoted as dim7 or °7, for example *F*#dim7 or *A*°7. The diminished is made by stacking two minor thirds together. This produces the 1-*b*3-*b*5. To make a dim7 we stack another minor third on top of the dim triad. This produces, in the key of C major, *B-D-F-Ab*. Something is wrong! There is no *A*b in the key of C major. Let's look at the interval chart with the *B* chromatic scale plugged in to see what is going on here.

B	C	Db	D	Eb	E	F	Gb	G	Ab	A	Bb	B
Root	m2	M2	m3	M3	P4	A4	P5	A5	M6	m7	M7	Octave

You can easily see the *B* and the *D*, but the *F* says that it's an augmented 4th. I thought this was a diminished chord? Here is where terminology comes in, again. The augmented 4th is the same thing as a diminished 5th. So, let me change the chart to reflect this.

B	C	Db	D	Eb	E	F	Gb	G	Ab	A	Bb	B
Root	m2	M2	m3	M3	P4	A4/d5	P5	A5	M6	m7	M7	Octave

Let's start over. We see the *B*, the *D*, and the F now, but the *A*b is a M6, not a seven at all. What is going on here?

Here is another rule. You can sharpen or flatten a note 2 times. This means that you can have a double sharp (##) or a double flat note (*bb*) (**NTS**). You will very rarely see these and you will <u>never</u> see a triple sharp or triple flat note, ever! This means that the *Ab* in the Bdim7 chord is in fact a *bb*7.

This means that a dim7 chord is 1-*b*3-*b*5-*bb*7. That isn't what we are playing though. When we use the C major scale starting on the 7th interval, B, we get *B-C-D-E-F-G-A*. Apply the shortcut 1-3-5-7 and this comes out to *B-D-F-A*. Look at the *B* chromatic scale interval chart. The *A* note is the m7. This means that in the key of C major there is a diminished chord that is 1-*b*3-*b*5-*b*7.

This is called a **half-diminished seventh chord**. This is more commonly referred to as a half-diminished chord. The notation for a half-diminished chord is m7*b*5 which means minor seventh flat five. The flat mark is a superscript on the left-hand side of the 5. This can be confusing just remember "flat 5". Notations for the half-diminished chord are min7(*b*5), m7(*b*5), or ᵒ̸. The last symbol is the degree symbol with a line through it, where the diminished seventh chord is a degree symbol without the line through it.

The diminished and the half-diminished have their special symbols added to the LCR numeration for the chord progressions. The diminished uses the degree symbol, °, and the half-diminished uses the degree symbol with a line through it, ᵒ̸. Some examples are iv ᵒ̸, or v°.

Now all I need to do is put a table up with all of the seventh chords in any major key.

Table 5-2:

Chord	Intervals	Chord type	symbol
1st	1-3-5-7	Major 7	M7, maj7, Δ
2nd	1-*b*3-5-*b*7	Minor 7	m7, min7, -7
3rd	1-*b*3-5-*b*7	Minor 7	m7, min7, -7
4th	1-3-5-7	Major 7	M7, maj7, Δ
5th	1-3-5-*b*7	Dominant 7	7
6th	1-*b*3-5-*b*7	Minor 7	m7, min7, -7
7th	1-*b*3-*b*5-*b*7	Half-diminished	min7(*b*5), m7(*b*5), ᵒ̸

Now we need to make the same chart, but this time we will construct it in the key of C major.

Table 5-3:

Chord	1st note	3rd note	5th note	7th note	1-3-5-7	Type of chord
1st	C	E	G	B	C-E-G-B	M7
2nd	D	F	A	C	D-F-A-C	min7
3rd	E	G	B	D	E-G-B-D	min7
4th	F	A	C	E	F-A-C-E	Dominant7
5th	G	B	D	F	G-B-D-A	Major
6th	A	C	E	G	A-C-E-G	minor
7th	B	D	F	A	B-D-F-A	diminished

We now know all of the seventh chords in the major scale and a weird one that isn't in the major scale (diminished seventh). There are two more seventh chords, but I am only going to mention one now, and the other will be discussed later in another chapter. The next seventh chord is oddly referred to as the **minor/major seventh chord**.

The minor/major seventh chord is written as –M7, –maj7, –m(maj7), or –Δ. The notes that make up the –M7 chord are 1-*b3*-5-7. This chord's name states exactly what it is. It's a minor chord with a major seventh on it.

Here are the barre chord types of seventh chords. Barre chords are moveable chords, so I will only put one type per string.

GM7

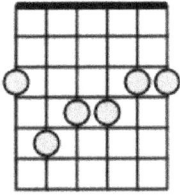

Gm7

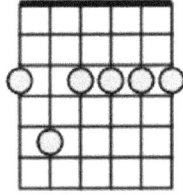

G7

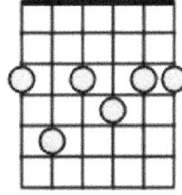

Gm7b5

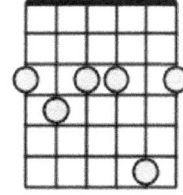

CM7

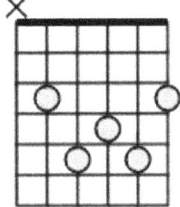

Cm7

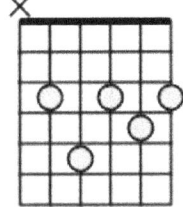

C7

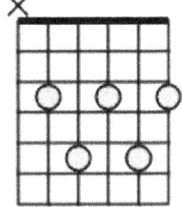

Cm7b5

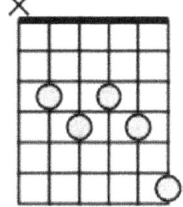

FM7

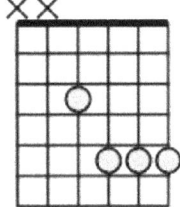

Fm7

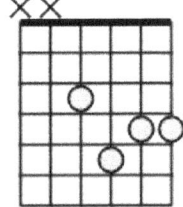

F7

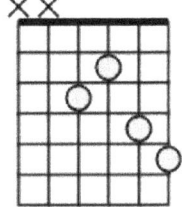

Fm7b5

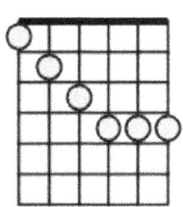

Half-diminished is also called minor7b5. There are more types of chords than you can shake a stick at. The next chapter will address the different kinds of chords, but not every single chord in existence. Once you get the theory down on making chords, you will be able to create many interesting varieties of chords.

Chapter 6

Altered Chords and Extended Chords

Many ideas have been discussed so far. Remember that they all build upon the previous chapters. The altered chords and extended chords are deviations or extensions of the chords that we have previously seen. The extension chords generally build large chords or chords with big intervals. The altered chords deviate from the methods that we have been accustomed to, thus far.

The extended chords add on to the seventh chords. If there are only 7 notes in a chord, how do you add more notes? This is interesting, to a degree (no pun intended). If we have a chord that is 1-3-5-7 we can add what is referred to as a 9, 11, or 13 to it. Where do these numbers come from?

Remember the octave (*8va*)? It is considered as the 1 or the 8, right? If we keep going we can say the 2nd becomes the 9th, the 4th becomes an 11th, and the 6th becomes a 13th. These notes are played above the octave. A maj9 chord is 1-3-5-7-9.

Not all of the notes have to be played. In extended chords some notes are eliminated from the chord. These are usually the 5, 7, 9 or 11.

If we were playing a **major ninth chord** like Cmaj9, we would play it as *C-E-G-B-D*. This correlates with the 1-3-5-7-9. A *C*9 chord is the **dominant 9th chord**. It has the same properties as a *C*7 chord with an added 9th. This would look like 1-3-5-b7-9 and the notes would be *C-E-G-Bb-D*. The C9 chord has a chord progression symbol of a superscript 9, i.e. I^9, IV^9, but 99% of the time it will be a V^9 chord. The dominant 9 chord in the major scale is the 5 chord. If we played a **minor ninth chord**, such as a *C*min9, it would be 1-b3-5-b7-9 and the notes would be *C-Eb-G-Bb-D*.

Of course these 3 types of chords may be in any key, but you wouldn't have a *C*maj9, *C*9, and a *C*min9 in the same scale. I am just doing it this way so you can see the differences between the types of chords. Use the same methods that we used in the chord theory and the seventh chord theory chapters.

If you played only the 1-3-5-9 and skipped the 7, this is called an **added 9th chord**. The notes for a *C*add9 chord are *C-E-G-D*.

Type of 9th chord	Intervals	Notes in key of C major
Maj9	1-3-5-7-9	C-E-G-B-D
9	1-3-5-b7-9	C-E-G-Bb-D
min9	1-b3-5-b7-9	C-Eb-G-Bb-D
added 9th	1-3-5-9	C-E-G-D

Here are some examples of the 9th chords.

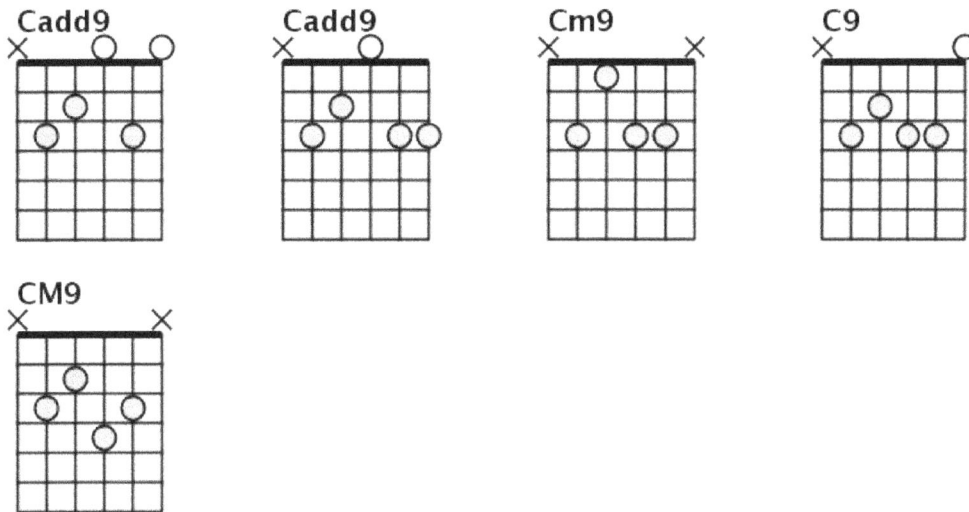

The 11th chords are seen mostly in Jazz music. They consist of an 11, which is the same degree as a 4th, an octave higher. The notes that are used in the 11th chords sometimes conflict with the major 3rd note that is present in the major triad. This would cause the conflict in the major 7 and dominant 7 type of 11th chord. The minor 3rd goes well with the 11th note.

We'll start with the minor 11th first then. The **minor11** carries the intervals 1-b3-5-b7-9-11. In C these notes would be C-Eb-G-Bb-D-F. That would probably be impossible to play on a guitar. The 5 and 9 notes can be eliminated to make playing the chord easier. This would give the intervals 1-b3-b7-11. In C this is C-Eb-Bb-F.

The major 11th will need some alteration or it will sound dissonant. To eliminate this dissonance the 11th is raised a half step to a #11th. This would give the **major7#11** the intervals 1-3-5-7-9-#11. In C this would be C-E-G-B-D-F#. The

5 and 9 notes are removed from this chord, like the minor11 chord. This yields the intervals 1-3-7-#11, which in C are C-E-B-F#.

The **dominant 11th** chord has the major 3rd in it, because remember it's a major chord. Thus, like before, we need to raise the 11 to #11 to eliminate the dissonance. This gives us the intervals 1-3-5-b7-9-#11. In C this would be C-E-G-Bb-D-F#. The 5 and 9 can be removed just like before to give us the 1-3-b7-#11 series of intervals. In C this amounts to C-E-Bb-F#.

Here is an example of each 11th chord.

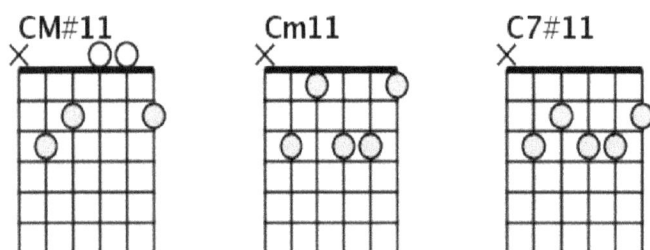

CM#11   Cm11   C7#11

A thing to note about the 11th chords: Some people will eliminate the dissonant major third from the major and dominant type of 11th chords. This makes the chord a suspended chord which will be discussed later. So, in 11 chords, the 3rd has to be present in the chord.

Another thing to keep in mind is the whole series of notes in this chord. For example, if I have a minor7#11 chord this can also appear to be a half-diminished chord. Think about it, the #4 is the same as a b5. The minor has a b3. We put that together it looks like 1-b3-b5-b7 which are the notes of a half-diminished chord. Here is the kicker though. It isn't a half-diminished chord because there is a 5 that can be played, but isn't being played.

As you probably have guessed, I like tables. So, let's have a table of all of the 11th chords that we have looked at.

Type of 11th chord	Intervals	Notes in key of C major
Maj7#11	1-3-5-7-9-#11	C-E-G-B-D-F#
11	1-3-5-b7-9-#11	C-E-G-Bb-D-F#
min7#11	1-b3-5-b7-9-#11	C-Eb-G-Bb-D-F#

The 13th chords are like the 9th and 11th type chords. We have the base triad, add the extensions 9 and 11, and then top it off with a 13th. This means that the intervals 1-3-5-7-9-11-13 are present. If we revert the 9 back to the 2, the 11 back to the 4, and the 13 back to the 6 we see 1-2-3-4-5-6-7. This means that all seven notes in the scale are present in the 13th chord.

In the 13th chord, just like before, the 5th and 9th intervals can be removed, but this time the 11th can be removed as well. This leaves the 1-3-7-13 intervals. Oddly enough, sometimes the 1 can be removed if there is a bass player which is playing the 1. Remember that because a note can be removed doesn't mean it has to be removed. That means if you keep the 11th in the chord the major and dominant types of chords having the major 3rd will have dissonance unless you introduce the #11.

The **major13** chord would have the intervals 1-3-7-13. The **minor13** chord would have the intervals 1-b3-b7-13. The **dom13** intervals are 1-3-b7-13.

Here are some common chords:

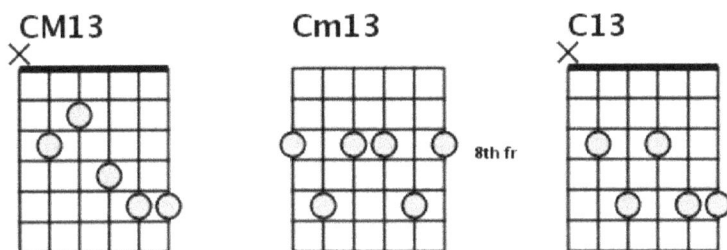

Here is a summary table:

Type of 13th chord	Intervals	Notes in key of C major
Maj13	1-3-7-13	C-E-B-A
13	1-3-b7-13	C-E-Bb-A
Min13	1-b3-b7-13	C-Eb-Bb-A

The 9th chords get used quite a bit, especially the Cadd9 and many other add9 chords. The 11th chords are found occasionally, but mainly in Jazz. The 13th chords are found even less and usually in Jazz music. This doesn't mean that you can't use them unless you play Jazz. Experiment and see what they sound like.

The **altered** series of chords are going to be used more that the extended in everyday situations. Understanding these will allow you to know what to play on top of them if you are soloing. It also helps in being creative. When writing a progression, put in a *D*sus2 chord instead of a regular *D*maj chord, or add in a *C*6/9 chord where there would be a *C*maj chord. The options are limitless.

Suspended chords are called suspended for a reason. The classical term meant that a note was carried from the previous chord into the chord and resolves on the tonic. That sounded complicated. Let me give you a more modern approach to the term suspended. The 3rd is the characteristic of a chord. If there is a *b*3 then it is minor. If a chord has a major 3rd then it is major. Say we eliminate the 3rd from the chord. Then we replaced the 3rd with another note. Is this chord major or minor? The answer is neither.

The suspended chords take a 2nd or 4th degree to replace the 3rd degree. With a triad it would look like 1-2-5 or 1-4-5 instead of 1-3-5 or 1-*b*3-5. Since there is no 3rd the characteristic of the chord is suspended. That isn't a textbook definition, but it helps to remember.

The **Suspended 4th** chords replace the 3rd with the 4th. They are usually referred to as "suspended" chords or "sus" chords. The **Suspended 2nd** chords are usually called "sus2" chords. They can sometimes be called suspended chords as well, which makes clarification an issue. The sus2 chords replace the 3rd with a 2nd.

Let's take a better look at these chords side-by-side.

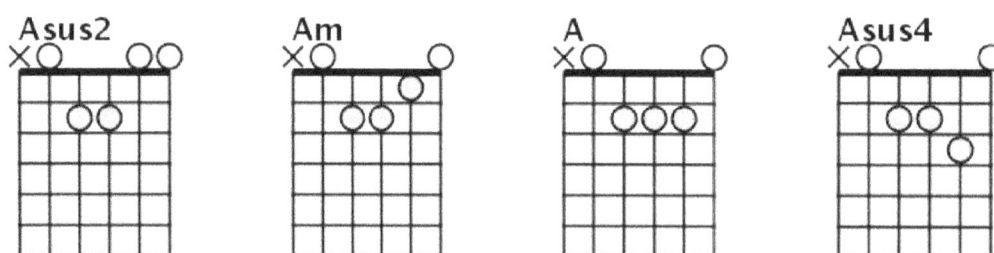

The difference between the *A*sus2, *A*m, *A*, and *A*sus4 in these chords is on the *B* string. If we take the notes of these in order we see *A*-**B**-*E, A*-**C**-*E, A*-**C#**-*E,* and *A*-**D**-*E.* The *A*sus2 or *A*sus4 chord can be played for either a major or minor chord. The weird thing about these is that you could play an *A* major or an *A* minor scale on top of the *A* suspended chords and they both work. That would make sense because these two chords have no 3rd making them neither major nor minor.

Sixth chords come in two varieties the major sixth chords and the minor sixth chords. Sixth (or 6) chords just add the 6th interval to the chord. The **major six** chords have the intervals 1-3-5-6, and the **minor six** chords have the intervals 1-b3-5-6. That's pretty simple. The major sixth in the key of *C* would be called a *C*6 chord. Notice that this is <u>not</u> a dominant chord. The minor sixth chord in the key of *E* is called a *C*min6 chord.

Examples of sixth chords are

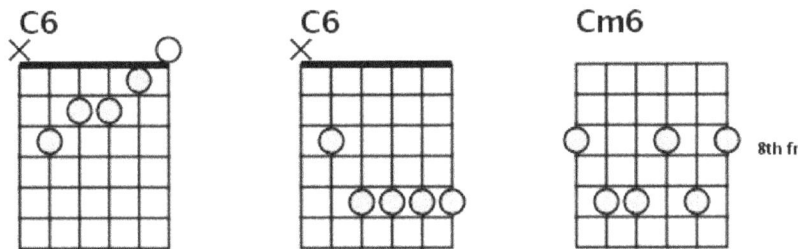

If you take the notes in the C6 chord C-E-G-A they are the same notes in the Am7 chord A-C-E-G, just inverted. This goes to show you that chords can be named more than one thing, and both names will be correct, depending on the context.

Chapter 7
Substitution Chords, Secondary Dominants, and Intermediary Chords

Chords, chords, chords! Why all of these sections about chords? Soloing is not the only thing in music. Ninety percent, if not more, of music is rhythm, and rhythm means chords.

I was playing in a music store where I taught a few years ago. There was an older gentleman, who had been a musician in the Army that would come in and play Jazz on a piano. I would ask questions about Jazz theory and he would answer them for me. He heard me playing one day and he told me, "You have all of the scales and playing down pat, but you don't have any chords." He insisted that I learn chords better, and then he said that I would have it all. I believe that to be an overstatement, but the point is that I needed more chord theory and chord utilization.

I made it a point to understand chords better, and teach on chords more, because chords *are* the song. The basic major minor chords will only work for so long and then you need to grow. This chapter covers using substitution chords and secondary dominants. This concept is pinnacle in Jazz music. It steps out of classical music theory a little, so hold on tight to your major scale.

Substitution chords do exactly that, they substitute one chord for another. This may not make sense, but it will soon enough. These are generally done in the seventh chord form. If you need more understanding of seventh chords, see the seventh chord chapter before continuing..

I am going to insert a chord table in key of *C* major for the seventh chords. Remember, that we build knowledge upon itself. Every time we move to a new subject you should see how the previous chapters contribute to the current chapter.

Table 7-1:

Chord	1st note	3rd note	5th note	7th note	1-3-5-7	Type of chord
1st	C	E	G	B	C-E-G-B	M7
2nd	D	F	A	C	D-F-A-C	min7
3rd	E	G	B	D	E-G-B-D	min7
4th	F	A	C	E	F-A-C-E	Dominant7
5th	G	B	D	F	G-B-D-A	Major
6th	A	C	E	G	A-C-E-G	minor
7th	B	D	F	A	B-D-F-A	diminished

I am going to take these chords and make a new table that puts these chords in a different order.

Table 7-2:

Chord	1st note	3rd note	5th note	7th note	1-3-5-7	Type of chord
1st	C	E	G	B	C-E-G-B	M7
3rd	E	G	B	D	E-G-B-D	min7
6th	A	C	E	G	A-C-E-G	minor
2nd	D	F	A	C	D-F-A-C	min7
4th	F	A	C	E	F-A-C-E	Dominant7
5th	G	B	D	F	G-B-D-A	Major
7th	B	D	F	A	B-D-F-A	diminished

From Table 7-2 we are going to see relationships. Music is all about relationships. Here we will use that knowledge. I have these chords grouped: 1st, 3rd, and 6th group, 2nd and 4th group, and the 5th and 7th group. These are substitution groups.

The 1st, 3rd, 6th group in the key of *C* has the chords: *C*maj7, *E*min7, and *A*min7 respectively. The 1st and 3rd share the notes *E*, *G*, and *B*.

1st	C	E	G	B	C-E-G-B	M7
3rd	E	G	B	D	E-G-B-D	min7

The 1st and 6th share the notes *C*, *E*, and *G*.

1st	C	E	G	B	C-E-G-B	M7
6th	A	C	E	G	A-C-E-G	min7

Notice the 3rd and 6th only share 2 notes, the *E* and the *G*.

3rd	E	G	B	D	E-G-B-D	min7
6th	A	C	E	G	A-C-E-G	min7

The 3rd (III) chord or the 6th (vi) chord can be substituted for the 1st (I) chord. The 1st can substitute in for a 3rd or a 6th. This means that where a I chord is, next time it's played, put in a III or vi. Or where there is a III or vi, plug in a I instead. This is a concept used in jazz. They take a turnaround and make substitutions to allow the song sound like it is making changes. A **turnaround** is when there are 3 or 4 chords that get played in a loop.

The most common turnaround in jazz is the I-vi-ii-V. These are all played as seventh chords which means that the I is a maj7 the vi is a min7 the ii is a min7 and the V is a dom7. Here is an example of playing this turnaround substituting for the I.

I-vi-ii-V / III-vi-ii-V / I-vi-ii-V

It wouldn't make sense to substitute the vi in for the I when the vi is the second chord in the progression. The slash (/) represents the next round. We can see that in 3 rounds we go from the I to the III back to the I. Usually there is only one substitution per round. This will evolve even more as we investigate the other substitution groups.

Look at the 2nd and 4th group. There are 3 notes that are similar, the *F, A,* and *C.*

2nd	D	F	A	C	D-F-A-C	min⁷
4th	F	A	C	E	F-A-C-E	Dominant7

These can be substituted for each other a ii for a IV, or a IV for a ii. Let's go back to the I-vi-ii-V progression again and plug in for the ii.

I-vi-ii-V / III-vi-ii-V / I-vi-VI-V / III-vi-VI-V

As you can see the more substitutions we get, the more options we have. We have one more substitution group. This is the 5th and 7th group. Both of these chords have tension. The use of a chord with tension normally follows a couple rules. Never end on a chord with **tension** because it sounds like it is going somewhere and never gets there.

The tension in these chords **resolves** with the tonic (I chord). Play a G7 chord then play a Cmaj7 behind it. It will sound like the G7 flows perfectly into the Cmaj7. The B ° chord is the same way. It resolves on the I. This feeling of resolution will come up a lot in music. So, you guessed it, *NTS*.

5th	G	B	D	F	G-B-D-A	Major
7th	B	D	F	A	B-D-F-A	½ dim

Here we will plug in for the new substitutions.

I-vi-ii-V / III-vi-ii-V / I-vi-VI-V / III-vi-VI-V / I-vi-ii-vii / III-vi-ii-V / I-vi-VI-vii / III-vi-VI-vii

I didn't add all of the permutations. Notice that the last chord is vii. If a chord has a diminished or dominant chord (tension chords) as the last chord it is automatically inferred that you know to put a I as the last chord, to resolve.

Try writing a progression in any key, find your substitution chords, and see what it sounds like when you do it. It doesn't have to be jazz, and you could even try it with base chords or power chords. Substitution is good knowledge. You will use this in music.

!!WARNING!!

This next topic moves out of classical theory (what we are studying) into jazz theory. These concepts are very important, but may confuse you if you don't have classical theory down yet. I suggest that if you are holding on by the seat of your pants at this stage to finish the book and come back to this section. In the aspect of the book as a whole, this is the most appropriate section to house this chapter, but from a learning aspect you might want to come back here later.

SECONDARY DOMINANTS

The next topic of discussion is called secondary dominants. The normal abbreviation for this is 2°. Secondary dominants build off of jazz turnarounds by inserting dominant seven chords where there aren't ones by normal chord theory. This in turn moves a chord progression through different keys. This means it will begin in a key, when the 2° is inserted the key changes, the key either returns to the original key, when removed, or changes to another key when another 2° is inserted.

First, let's use a normal jazz turnaround, ii-V-I. This progression is built backwards by 5's. If we start with I, we count up 5 and get the V chord (remember I is 1). We place this behind the I chord and get V-I. If we count up 5 from V we get a ii, and place that behind the V and get ii-V-I. Now if we kept going, the next chord, up 5 from ii, gets us to vi. Then we would have vi-ii-V-I. Go up 5 from vi and we get a III, then the progression is III-vi-ii-V-I. If you look at the substitution section above, the I-vi-ii-V progression should come to mind.

Now, back to ii-V-I. We can see that we are adding chords to the progression by going up a 5th from the previous chord. If you don't get what I am saying, recall that there are seven chords and that they will constantly loop. Here is a table:

C	D	E	F	G	A	B	C	D	E	F	G	A	B	C	D
I	ii	iii	IV	V	vi	vii	I	ii	iii	IV	V	vi	vii	I	ii

If we used this table with the ii-V-I example, we see that *C* is the I. We go up 5 chords to *G* which is the V and we place it before the I making V-I. We then go up 5 chords from *G* and get *D* which is a ii chord. We put that before the V and get ii-V-I.

The concept here is 5. We know that the V chord is a dom7 chord. The dom7 is normally labeled V^7. We take the other UCR numerals and LCR numeration at face value that I is maj7, ii is min7, iii is min7, IV is maj7, vi is min7, and vii is half-diminished. The V is the only one that uses the superscript 7 to indicate dom7. If I had a IV^7 that would indicate in the key of *C* an *F*7 chord, even though diatonically the IV is a maj7 chord.

So, the ii-V-I is really ii-V^7-I. We take the idea of secondary dominant, which means that the ii being the 5 of the V is now a II^7, the dominant of the dominant, hence the secondary dominant, making the chord progression now II^7-V^7-I. We can turn this wheel in full circle. Let's make secondary dominants in the key of *C* all the way through from I.

First let's figure out the chords, then write them down.

I-V-ii-vi-iii-vii-IV-I

Write them backwards.

I-IV-vii-iii-vi-ii-V-I

Before the next step, play the progression and hear how it sounds. Now, let's make them secondary dominants.

I-IV^7-VII^7-III^7-VI^7-II^7-V^7-I

Play that progression. Now you can play **ii-V^7-I / II^7-V^7-I** and so on.

Plug this in the I-vi-ii-V and get

I-vi-ii-V / I-vi-II^7-V^7 / I-VI^7-II^7-V^7 / III^7-VI^7-II^7-V^7 and etc.

INTERMEDIARY DIMINISHED OR DOMINANT CHORDS

Intermediary diminished or dominant chords are another jazz move. This gets kind of interesting that we make diminished chords that are in between chords when moving up a progression linearly and dominant seventh chords when moving down a progression linearly.

If we have a progression that goes I-ii-iii-V⁷-I we have a series of linear chords (I-ii-iii). A way to embellish this "walk" upwards is by using diminished seventh in between the I, ii, and iii chords. By this I mean that we would have a *b*ii° and *b*iii° added to the progression. This would give us I-*b*ii°-ii-*b*iii°-iii-V⁷-I.

Let me write out the chords in the key of *C* for you. First, without the diminished and then with the diminished chords added.

Cmaj7 - Dmin7 – Emin7 - G7 - Cmaj7

Cmaj7 - C#° - Dmin7 - D#° - Emin7 - G7 - Cmaj7

We can even add a dim7 chord after the *E*min7 if we so desire, but that would encroach on the Fmaj7 that is in the chord. It can still be done though

Let me give you the chords I usually use in that specific progression.

TAB 7-1:

The dim7 acts as a leading chord for the next chord. The dim7 causes tension (dissonance) that is resolved (consonance) in the following chord. The chords themselves are referred to as passing chords. These passing chords are common in linear progression, which is what we are doing. Think of a passing chord as a territory that is out of bounds, yet we are passing through briefly to get to where we are going, for instance, cutting through your neighbor's back yard in order to get to your buddy's house.

This type of diminished leading chord can be referred to as the supertonic leading diminished seventh chord. This means that the tonic (the root note *C* in this case) is sharpened (*C#*) and leads to the supertonic which is another term for the ii chord.

When moving backwards in a linear progression, or downward, the dominant seventh can be used to create the same effect as before. I will demonstrate with the key of *C*.

iii-ii-I-V⁷-I

Now add the dominant seventh chords in between the linear chords iii-ii-I. This will produce the progression:

iii-bIII⁷-ii-bII⁷-I-V⁷-I

Emin7   Eb7   Dmin7   Db7   Cmaj7   G7   Cmaj7

The dom7 chords move the progression down. Play the passage and listen to how the chord progression has a falling down effect.

Chapter 8
Arpeggios

Arpeggios have been the growing trend in music because of the sweep. A sweep is an arpeggio that is played fast and the guitarist picks down or up the strings in a sweeping motion.

The term arpeggio is an Italian that means "broken chord". This brokenness is the succession of the notes in a chord rather than the strumming of the notes in a chord. An arpeggio doesn't have to be a sweep or a melodic interlude, but it can be a rake of a chord.

This raking is where the chord isn't strummed where all note tones are heard at the same time, but the notes are played one-by-one in a chord shape like usual, but the notes are sustained to hold out like a chord. There is an interesting marking to signify this type of arpeggiation. Notice how Example 1 shows arpeggiation, but the notation above it doesn't. The true notation version is Example 2 in TAB 8-1.

The form of arpeggiation that is most prevalent these days consists of individual notes of a chord played successively. The usual method uses a triad and plays the notes concurrently, not out of order. This is normally in the form 1-3-5. Arpeggios can be major, minor, diminished, augmented, seventh, or whatever. If you don't understand chord theory, this section will start to get confusing. Go back to the scale theory and chord theory chapters and review.

Major triads consist of a 1-3-5 from the major scale. In the key of *C* this would be *C-E-G*. If we played this as an arpeggio it could have different shapes because a *C*maj chord can be played as a chord many different ways. The most widely used shapes or forms are the *A*, *D*, and *E* shape.

The *A* shape comes directly from the *A* major barre chord.

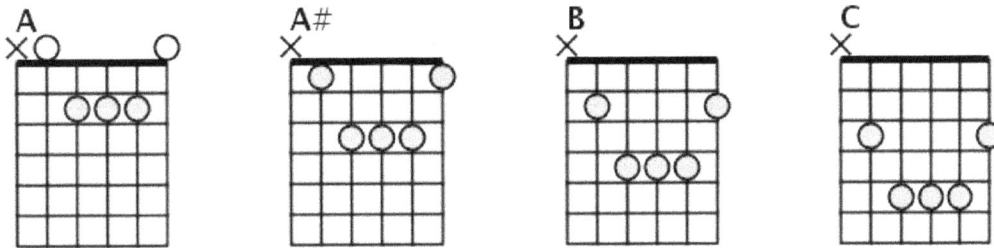

The problem with a regular *A* shaped chord is that it doesn't go in the form 1-3-5. It follows a 1-5-1-3-5 pattern if we play the chord one note at a time. Therefore, we need to add in a 3 after the 1 and before the 5 to make this follow the desired pattern. All of the following chord shapes will be adjusted to meet the criteria of 1-3-5.

TAB 8-1 illustrates the basic *A* shaped arpeggio. The arpeggio is a *C* major. The shape is *A* major, because it looks like the open *A* major chord. The stretch on this is quite large. Up the neck, at the second octave (15th fret) it's much easier. Remember, these are moveable shapes. If this was on the 4th fret of the *A* string, it would be a *C#* major arpeggio. If it were on the 5th fret of the *A* string, it would be a *D* major arpeggio, and so on.

The arpeggio doesn't need to start on the 1, end on the 1, or be in order. That is just the way that most guitarists play them. You can try playing this arpeggio starting on the *E* or *G* if you like.

Arpeggios can be *A* minor shaped as well. These look like the open *A* minor chord. I will add the extra note to the *A* minor chord shape to make it follow 1-b3-5. In *C* this would be *C-Eb-G*.

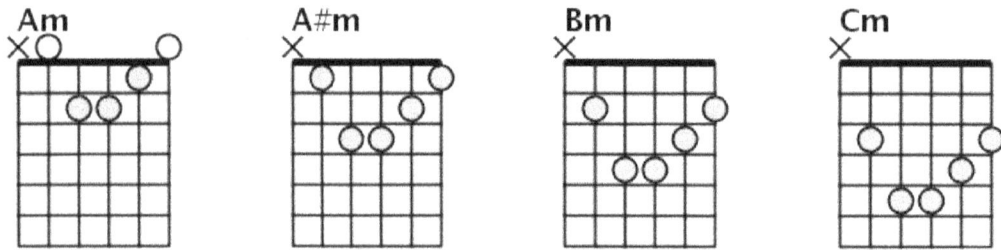

Am

A#m

Bm

Cm

TAB 8-3 illustrates the basic *A* minor shaped arpeggio. The arpeggio is a *C* minor.

TAB 8-3:

The next arpeggio shape is the *D* shape. This is the most used shape. It's called the *D* shape because it coincides with the *D* open chords, such as *D* major, *D* minor, etc. The *D* shape is a bit different than the *A* shape because the *D* shape appears to be different than the normal *D* chord that we play every day. In actuality, it looks more like a *C* chord than a *D* chord. The following chords are in the *D* shape. Note the 1st chord is a standard *D* and the 2nd one is the *D* shape arpeggio form.

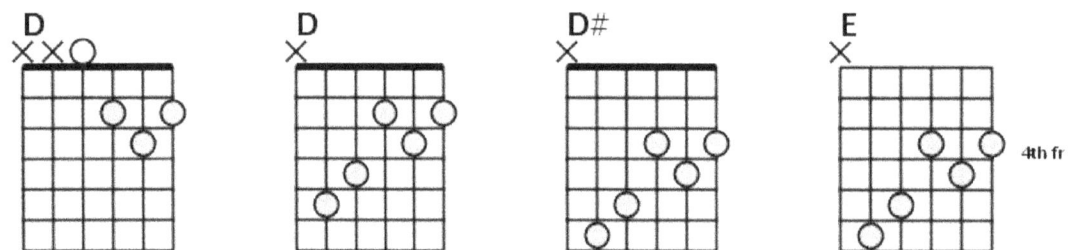

D

D

D#

E

4th fr

TAB 8-4:

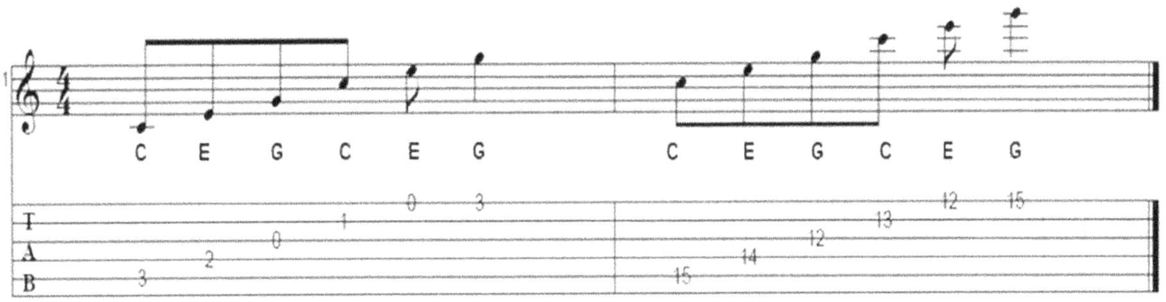

TAB 8-4 shows the *C* major arpeggio in the *D* shape. One *C* major arpeggio is an octave higher. This form as you can see ends on the *G* and not the *C*.

The D minor shaped arpeggios are next. Remember these arpeggios are in *C*.

TAB 8-5:

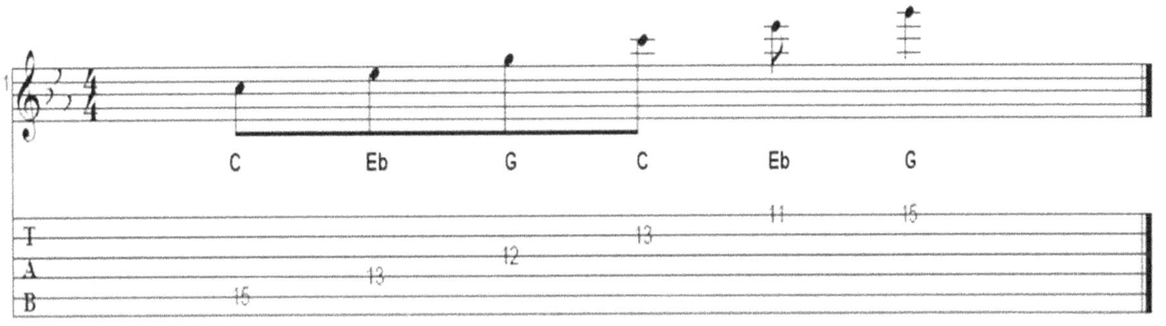

In TAB 8-5 the *Eb* would be below the open *E* string, so I only entered the TAB for the 2nd octave.

The last shape commonly used is the *E* shape. This is the least used of the three shapes shown here. The *E* shape coincides with the open *E* chords. These are not in the 1-3-5 form. They are in 1-5-1-3-5-1, so I will adjust it in the TAB.

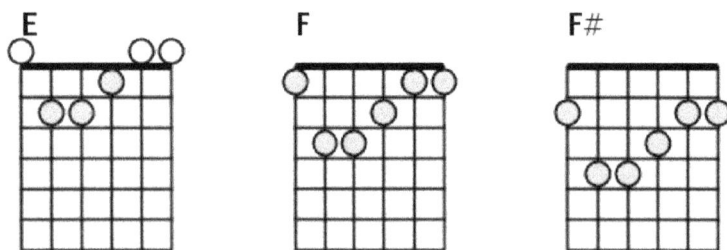

E   F   F#

TAB 8-6:

The *E* minor shape is as you would expect by now, in the shape of an *E* minor chord.

TAB 8-7:

Now that we have the concept of what they are and what they look like, the obvious question is how they are used. An arpeggio can be used in many formats. If a chord progression of I-IV-V was being played in the key of C, then one could play the I arpeggio over the I chord to produce a melody over the chord. This could be done for the IV and V chords in the progression as well.

You could solo with an arpeggio. For example if the rhythm was playing a chord progression with the I-IV-V progression as stated above, the soloist could either play a scale and go into an arpeggio, play a scale, arpeggio then a scale again, or play all arpeggios over the chord progression.

Exercise 8-1:

Exercise 8-1 shows a scale-arpeggio-scale type of run that could be incorporated over a chord progression. Of course, this is just a basic run for information purposes. Notice the *C* major scale is not in order. A scale doesn't need to be played one note after the other and sound like a scale, although the last measure has the *C* major scale played backwards.

Exercise 8-2 shows a vi-iii chord progression in the key of *C*. Guitar 2 plays an *A* minor arpeggio in 2 different octaves, the first being the *D* shaped and the second octave arpeggio is the bottom half of the *Am* shaped arpeggio form. The second measure plays the *E* shaped *E* minor arpeggio. Notice that the *E* minor arpeggio doesn't start on *E*, nor does it start on the *E* string. This arpeggio starts at the bottom half of the arpeggio and then works its way back up to the lower *E*.

Exercise 8-2:

When playing arpeggios, play different ones back to back, like when you studied chords. Listen how they sound together. Try playing arpeggios in a key diatonically (I-ii-iii-IV-V-vi-vii). Then try playing in patterns. I like the pattern of 4ths. Here is an example that follows the pattern of 4ths.

Example 8-3:

The pattern: ii-vi-I-iv

Try thirds, sixths, etc. See what _you_ like.

TAB 8-8:

TAB 8-8 shows the diatonic arpeggios in the key of C. Note that these go exactly with the chords in the key of C. If the chords in a major scale are always M-m-m-M-M-m-d, then the arpeggios should be the same because an arpeggio is a broken chord. Keep it simple. Look for relationships and similarities.

There is a lot of stock, here lately, in the arpeggio. If you're "somebody" on the guitar you know arpeggios. The problem that I see in most people is that they spend so much time learning scales, licks, and arpeggios, but very few ever want to spend the time to learn the theory behind it. Understanding the theory behind the music allows you to be more creative.

Take the time to think of the chords being arpeggiated and the underlying chord that is being played. My next chapter will utilize the idea of mode theory. This will allow you to play all sorts of ideas that you never would have played before. More information about arpeggios can be found in my book, "Exotic Scales and Arpggios".

Chapter 9
Modes

Mode theory is where we take a scale and use every note as a starting point. This in turn will allow for special step progressions between the notes which give the linear arrangement a different sound. These step progressions are unique to the type of mode, just as the W-W-H-W-W-W-H step progression is uniquely the major scale. There are 7 modes in total:

Table 9-1:

Mode	Step Progression
Ionian	W-W-H-W-W-W-H
Dorian	W-H-W-W-W-H-W
Phrygian	H-W-W-W-H-W-W
Lydian	W-W-W-H-W-W-H
Mixolydian	W-W-H-W-W-H-W
Aeolian	W-H-W-W-H-W-W
Locrian	H-W-W-H-W-W-H

Wait a minute… I just said that the major scale is unique? The Ionian mode is the same thing as the major scale? The Ionian scale is the major scale. This will become apparent soon.

The concept of a mode is the same as the concept of making chords. We start with the first note of the key and make the scale, go to the next note of the key and make the next scale, and so on. Here is a visual to make it easy.

Table 9-2:

Mode	Step Progression	Notes in the key of C
Ionian	W-W-H-W-W-W-H	C-D-E-F-G-A-B-C
Dorian	W-H-W-W-W-H-W	D-E-F-G-A-B-C-D
Phrygian	H-W-W-W-H-W-W	E-F-G-A-B-C-D-E
Lydian	W-W-W-H-W-W-H	F-G-A-B-C-D-E-F
Mixolydian	W-W-H-W-W-H-W	G-A-B-C-D-E-F-G
Aeolian	W-H-W-W-H-W-W	A-B-C-D-E-F-G-A
Locrian	H-W-W-H-W-W-H	B-C-D-E-F-G-A-B

This should look familiar. This is how we made chords. The step progression is the main factor here, not the notes. The notes coincide with the steps, but it is the whole-steps and the half-steps that are important in modes.

The first thing that we need to do is recall some information. Do you remember the major and minor chords in order diatonically in the major scale? It goes M-m-m-M-M-m-d. The theory builds on itself. If you don't have this knowledge go back through the chapters and become familiar with these concepts first, then return.

If the ii chord in the key of *C* is *D* minor, it would make sense to say that the 2nd mode in *C* is a *D* minor mode. This is true, but you will learn that the term "minor" is stated loosely here. It is minor in the sense that the 3rd is flattened from its corresponding major scale, but you will learn that the minor scale is a unique scale as well. So, in a major or minor 3rd aspect the scales follow the same M-m-m-M-M-m-d pattern as the chords. This is justified by looking at the step pattern.

In the Ionian (major) we see the W-W-H-W-W-W-H this is clearly the major scale. The term *C* major scale and *C* Ionian mode are interchangeable, but most prefer the first rather than the latter. The second mode, the **Dorian**, has a step progression of W-H-W-W-W-H-W. This is clearly different than the major scale. It is still in the same key as the Ionian mode because it uses the same notes as the Ionian. It is the second permutation (if you will) of the Ionian mode. Let me make a table to visualize the concept (Table 9-3).

Table 9-3:

D major scale (Ionian)	D	E	F#	G	A	B	C#
D Dorian mode	D	E	F	G	A	B	C
Note difference			b3				b7

We can see by the previous table that the *D* Dorian mode has a *b*3 and *b*7 as compared to its major scale. Note that it is in the key of C, but we always refer back to the major scale of the mode in question to explain its properties. This is a bit confusing, but easily explainable. You have to make a comparison for there to be a standard and an alteration. If I have D-E-F-G-A-B-C or D-E-F#-G-A-B-C# or D-E-F#-G#-A-B-C# which one is the standard? The D major scale is the standard, and how other scales are arranged that differ from the major scale are the altered scales.

Just so you know, the Dorian mode step progression is the same for every Dorian mode in all keys. The Dorian mode has a *b*3 and *b*7. If you play a scale with this characteristic, it is a Dorian mode. I could have easily said that if you play the *C* major scale starting on the *D* that is a *D* Dorian mode. It's pretty much that simple.

The next mode is the **Phrygian mode**. This mode has the *b*3 giving it the characteristics of a minor chord, yet it has a *b*2 and *b*6 as well, giving it a Middle Eastern sound. Of course Table 9-4 will show you how it compares to the major scale.

Table 9-4:

E major scale (Ionian)	E	F#	G#	A	B	C#	D#
E Phrygian mode	E	F	G	A	B	C	D
Note difference		b2	b3			b6	b7

The Phrygian mode has a *b*2, *b*3, *b*6, and *b*7 as compared to its major scale; easily visible with the table. Remember, this is in the key of *C* major. If it were in the key of *D* major, the Phrygian mode would be an *F#* Phrygian mode, not *E* Phrygian. This is because the third note in the key of *D* major is *F#* not *E*.

So, in the key of *C* major there are 7 notes and there are 7 permeations of the major scale that coincide with the 7 modes. These modes are the Ionian, Dorian, Phrygian, Lydian, Mixolydian, Aeolian, and the Locrian. Table 9-2 shows all of the modes.

If you have never seen The Sound of Music, this may not make sense. The Ionian has the Do-Re-Mi-Fa-So-La-Ti-Do sound (each sound refers to a note of the scale: Do = C, Re = D, Mi = E, etc. Research: solfege). The Dorian is Re-Mi-Fa-So-La-Ti-Do-Re, the Phrygian is Mi-Fa-So-La-Ti-Do-Re-Mi, and etc.

I will now attempt to explain a couple methods of using the modes. Do not forget that these modes are all in the same key.

Let's peruse the musical realm for a minute and suppose that we are playing a song with the progression I-IV-V in the key of *G*. This means of course that we are playing *G*, *C*, and *D* in that very order. Also note that these are all major chords. Now, let's go out on a limb and say you are playing a solo on top of this 3 chord progression. What can you do?

There are many options, but most people would play an E minor pentatonic scale until I was ready to throw them out of the window. That is not what we want to do.

I would look at this in a couple different ways. I could either view this progression as a whole or in individual pieces. By that I mean, I could view it as it being in the key of *G* major, or I could view it as a *G* maj chord, *C* maj chord, and a *D* maj chord. I have more options with the second scenario, but first I will start with viewing it as a whole.

The majority of individuals (besides the pentatonic people) would play *G* major through and through. This can be a bit monotonous. The modes allow us to play where we stay in the key, yet we are able to break the monotony. Over the first round of the progression, I could play a melody in *G* major (Ionian). The next time it changes to *C*, I could play a *C* Lydian, then into a *D* Mixolydian over the *D* major chord. I could continue to play the *D* Mixolydian mode through the entirety of the next round of chords.

As you can see the options go from one scale to 3 modes. Many people play modes and never know it. The second approach can get more complicated. Let's assume that we are only playing 3 chords, not extended chords. We know that the *G* major has a *G-B-D* in it. This means that there are 9 notes not being played out of the chromatic scale and 4 notes not being played out of the G major scale. This statement is true for the other 2 chords as well, but their notes are *C-E-G* and *D-F-A*.

Over the *G* we could play a *G* Ionian, over the C we could play either a *C* Lydian or a *C* major scale, and over the *D* we could play a *D* Mixolydian or a *D* major scale. This method involves key centers and more theory, but the idea should be straight forward. If you are playing over a *C* major scale, there is no difference between playing in any key that involves a *C* major chord. Why? Because the ear hears a *C* chord not a *G* major key. Don't get caught up in being forced into the key of the song, but the key of the chord playing at that moment.

There are going to be (usually) 3 keys that will harbor any 1 chord. The *C* major for example is in the key of *C* (obviously), *G*, and *F*. How did I know that? Well we do know that the chord progression for any major key is M-m-m-M-M-m-d. This means there are only 3 places that a major chord could be, either the I the IV or the V (look where the "M" is), thus I looked for a key where the *C* was in those places.

In the key of *C* we have a *C* Ionian, in the key of *G* we have a *C* Lydian, and in the *F* we have a *C* Mixolydian. These are quite different though. Take a look at Table 9-5.

Table 9-5:

C Ionian	C	D	E	F	G	A	B
C Lydian	C	D	E	F#	G	A	B
C Mixolydian	C	D	E	F	G	A	Bb

These three scales will noticeably sound different (because they are in 3 different keys), maybe not by a large margin because we can see the relationship between them. Strum a *C* major and play the *C* Ionian, then strum the chord again and play the *C* Lydian, then strum one more time and play the *C* Mixolydian. You will notice a subtle difference in the sound of the three scales, but they will all play over the *C* major just fine. If you don't know how to play these modes I will list them in order.

C Ionian

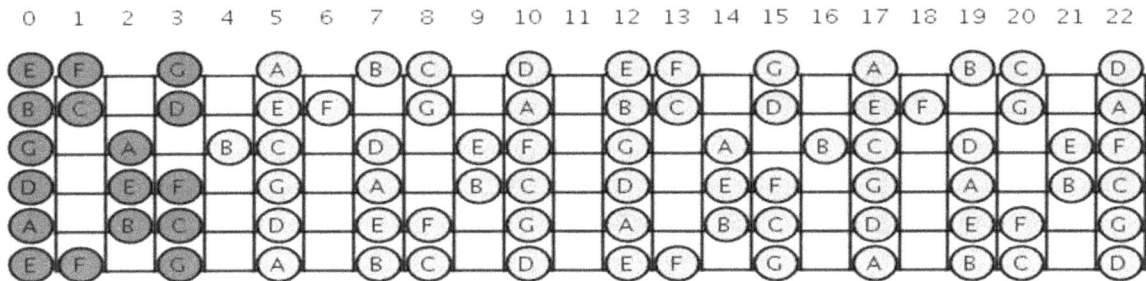

C Lydian

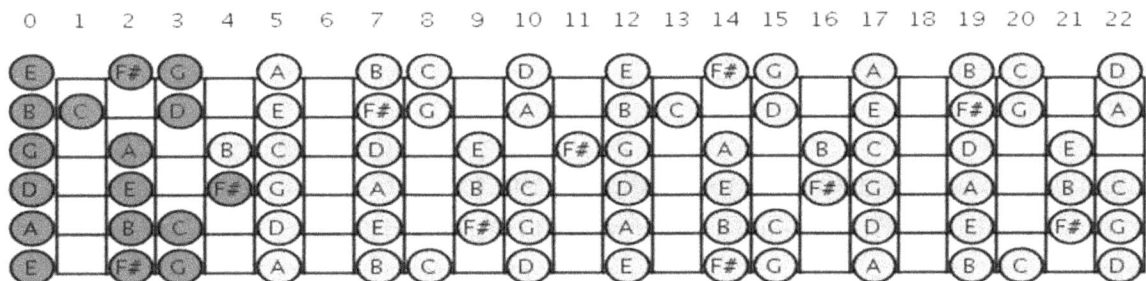

C Mixolydian

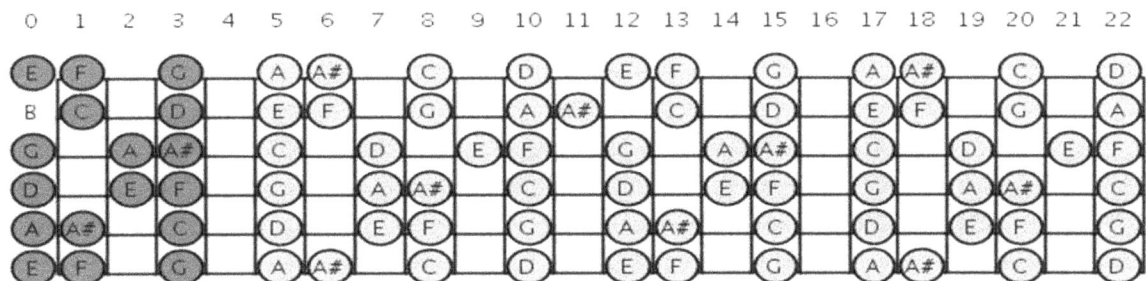

In using these diagrams, just find a *C* (i.e. 3rd fret *A* string or 10th fret *E* string) and build a scale that you feel comfortable playing. This is how I "make" scales. I get a diagram of the notes and I find the root note, then I play the notes in a way that I like the best. There is no set scale. Many books list a scale and say, "play this scale". I find it better to have you choose how you want to play the scale.

I find this to be the best way to play over a progression. Let's use a minor chord in a progression and see what we can come up with. The next progression is

I-vi-ii-V in the key of *D*. This would mean that the chord progression is D-Bm-Em-A. What modes could we play over the Em?

The answer is the *E* Dorian, *E* Phrygian, and/or the *E* Aeolian. Let's compare these modes Table 9-6. Remember that *D* major naturally has 2 sharps (*C#* and *F#*).

Table 9-6:

E Dorian	E	F#	G	A	B	C#	D
E Phrygian	E	F	G	A	B	C	D
E Aeolian	E	F#	G	A	B	C	D

You can tell that they are quite similar. That shouldn't be too big of a surprise. I found these the same way as I found the major modes. I looked my chord mantra M-m-m-M-M-m-d. Take a look at the m's, they are either at the ii, iii, or vi position. This means I need to pick scales where the *E* is in those positions. *D* major has *E* as the ii (*D-E-F#-G-A-B-C#-D*), *C* major has E as the iii (*C-D-E-F-G-A-B-C*), and *G* major has *E* as the vi (*G-A-B-C-D-E-F#-G*).

E Dorian

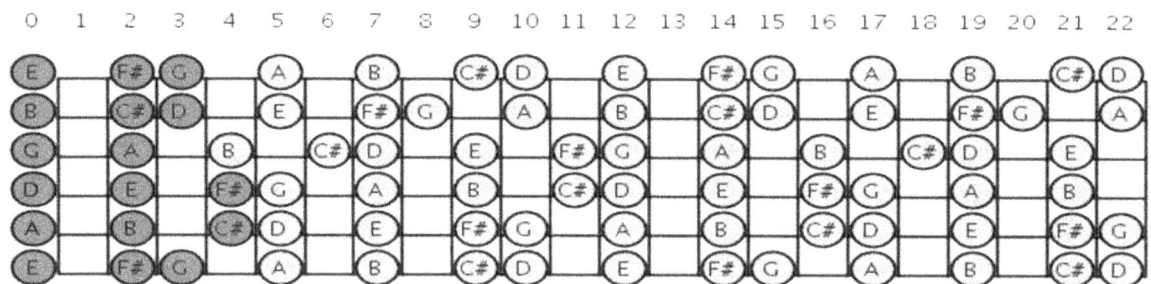

E Phrygian

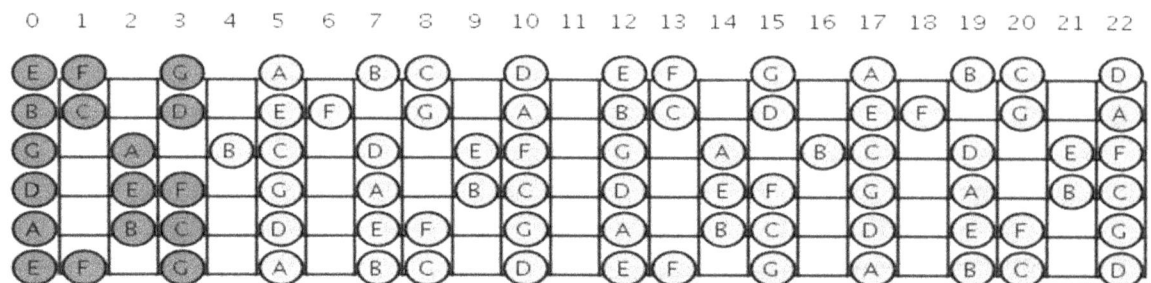

E Aeolian

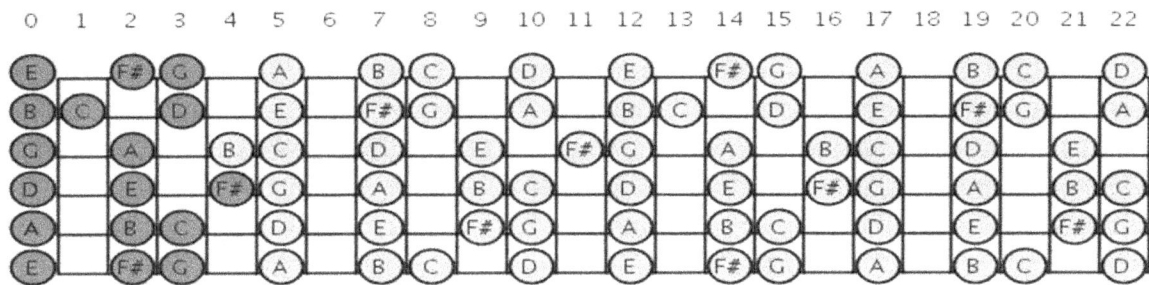

This may seem convoluted, but it isn't. If you expect to read this from cover to cover and "get it", it's not going to happen. You are going to have to get out that paper and pencil like I had spoken about earlier and do some work. If you don't write this stuff down, it may take you much more time to understand.

You write this down by finding the chord of interest, in the last case Em. Then you need to write down the chord mantra M-m-m-M-M-m-d. Since the Em is a minor chord the mode will be a "minor type" chord. This is at the ii, the iii, and the vi. If it is a ii, it's a Dorian, right? Look at Table 9-2. One letter before *E* is *D*, that makes it in the key of *D* and you have an *E* Dorian. The iii is in the key of *C* because 2 notes before *E* is *C*. The iii is a Phrygian meaning that the iii is the *E* Phrygian. The vi is the Aeolian making it the *E* Aeolian which is in the key of *G*. 2 notes after *E* is *G* (6-7-8, 8 = 1), therefore the *E* Aeolian is in the key of *G* major. It's that easy. The hard part is playing it how you want to. Finding it is the easy part.

WHAT WE LEARNED:

♪ There are 7 modes

♪ These modes are unique in that the step progression clearly defines it.

♪ The modes are permutations of the major scale

♪ We can play over a chord progression either by looking at it as a whole or by looking at is as individual parts.

♪ We can play modes over the entire chord progression or over corresponding chords.

♪ We must use more than our imagination to grasp these concepts. We need to use paper and pencil to write out the formulas.

Here is a question to ponder. What mode(s) can you play over both the Bm and the Em?

First find the notes in both chords.

Next, determine which modes have all of these notes.

Hint: There are quite a few modes that will work note wise, but the real question is which ones sound good over the chords. That is to be determined by the context by which the chords are played and what you are trying to get out of it. It's all in how you want it to sound. That's where the freedom comes in. You are free to make it sound as good or as bad as you want.

Using modes to the fullest:

Modes can be just as boring if played in a boring manner. Let me give you an example. Your buddy is playing a progression that involves a *G* chord, so you decide to be cool and play a *G* Mixolydian over that part of the progression. That would be cool, but there could be other alternatives to playing over that *G* chord.

For sake of argument, let's just assume that the guitarist is just jamming out a *G* chord for you to play a solo over. This will be the easiest way to start out, and then we will branch into harder progressions. This *G* chord has 3 notes *G-B-D*, and that's all.

Let's look at the chords in *G* major. Use the chord mantra M-m-m-M-M-m-d. Thus we have:

Table 9-7:

Chord	1st note	3rd note	5th note	1-3-5	Type of chord
1st	G	B	D	G-B-D	Major
2nd	A	C	E	A-C-E	minor
3rd	B	D	F#	B-D-F#	minor
4th	C	E	G	C-E-G	Major
5th	D	F#	A	D-F#-A	Major
6th	E	G	B	E-G-B	minor
7th	F#	A	C	F#-A-C	diminished

This will reveal the scales, modes, and arpeggiated chord shapes that are in the key. We can see in Table 9-7 that the 3rd chord favors the 1st chord. This is an idea we covered on substitution chords. The 6th chord is also very similar in that the 3rd and 6th chords share 2 of the 3 notes in the *G* maj chord.

This is interesting in that we will be playing off of minor scales on top of a major chord. Playing off of the 1 is fine and dandy, but playing off of other notes in the chord tends to bring out other qualities of the chord. I like playing off of the 3 in a chord because it supports the chord without reaffirming the fact that it is a *G* chord.

This is what I am saying. When someone is playing a chord, and in this case it's a *G* maj, I would play the B Phrygian, where I am playing off of the *B* (3rd) in the chord instead of the *G*. Everybody hears *G* then starts a run in *G* and ends on *G*. Try not thinking like that and see what comes out. You could also play off of the *D* (5th) by playing a *D* Mixolydian. You could even end on these notes over the chord. The 3rd sounds better than the 5th does though. Another idea would be to play an arpeggio off of the chord. The Bm and D maj arpeggio is an example of what I just stated above.

I also tend to play the relative minor over the major. In this case the relative minor would be the *E* minor. This is the same thing as the *E* Aeolian mode. As stated above, the Em has 2 of the same notes as the *G* maj chord, thus if you arpeggiated an Em over a *G* chord it would sound good.

Now, the concept of a progression with more than one chord is the same as with one chord. We can view all of the chords as a whole or individually like we have done previously. The progression is *Em-C-G-D*. This is in the key of *G*. I know this because in the sharp keys only 2 keys have a *C* as opposed to a *C#*. These are the keys of *G* and *C*. *C* has a *D*m not a *D* chord as the ii. That leaves the G. I guess C is not either a flat or a sharp key, so then only one key fits. Only one flat key has an E and that's the key of F. The key of F has a Gm and Dm and E °, so it doesn't fit at all. You should be able to figure the keys out by now.

Here are the options that I would play over the entire progression or parts of it:

E Aeolian, G Ionian, C Ionian, C Lydian, D Ionian, D Mixolydian, E Phrygian, **A** Dorian, **A** Aeolian, B Phrygian, C arpeggio, D arpeggio, Em arpeggio, G arpeggio, **A**m arpeggio, Bm arpeggio, E ° arpeggio, and various other minors and ragas that we haven't covered.

I would play some of these over specific chords or groups of chords. Some can be played over the entire progression. Remember, you can move out of the key of the progression if you remain true to the chords being played. This is more along the idea of Jazz Theory rather than Classical Theory.

Chapter 10
Minor Scales / Minor Keys

The minor scale is a loose term. There are 3 minor scales used throughout most music. There are also 3 modes that have a *b*3 making them have minor characteristics. Any scale that has a *b*3 is a minor scale. The term "minor scale" usually refers to the **natural minor scale**.

The natural minor scale is the same thing as the Aeolian mode. That is why the mode theory chapter comes before minor scale theory. You would be inclined to think that this should be a short chapter, but like usual there is always more to the story.

The notes in the *A* natural minor scale are *A-B-C-D-E-F-G*. This should be the easiest scale of all to memorize. It can be played a million different ways. Here is a scale diagram for *A* Aeolian.

A Aeolian

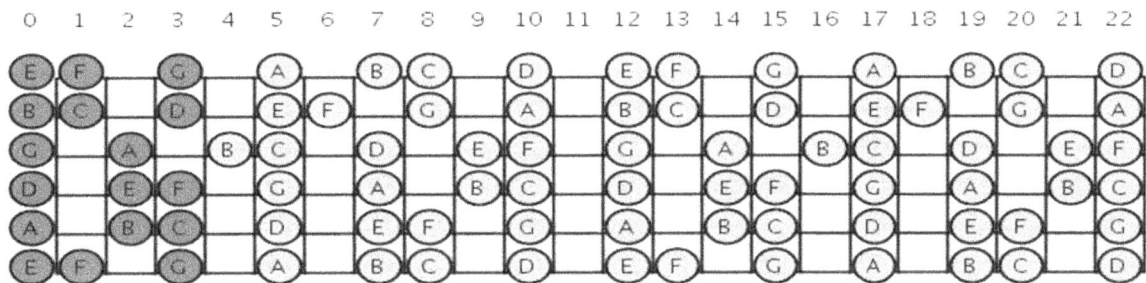

This brings up two other concepts, relative minors and minor keys. Relative minors are the Aeolian modes of a major key. In the key of *C* major, the relative minor is *A* minor. In the key of *G* major, the relative minor is E minor. If you think about it, when you play in *E* minor, you really play in *G* major. That's why I teach so much in *G* and *C*. These two major scales will be played more than any other scales. The keys of *G*, *C*, Am, and Em make up a majority of all songs.

The minor keys are explained as thus, there is I-IV-V in the major keys, but if you start a progression in the natural minor scale you can have a i-iv-v in the minor key. That is why the vi is used instead of the ii or iii, because this wouldn't be possible if they were the key centers.

We need to see the chord mantra to get this visualized. M-m-m-M-M-m-d is used for major, and m-d-M-m-m-M-M is used for the minor keys. Clearly these are different, but it allows us to have i-iv-v and they are all minor chords. That's my quick and dirty explanation.

Table 10-1:

Major Key (Sharps)	Relative Minor
C	Am
G	Em
D	Bm
A	F#m
E	C#m
B	G#m
F#	D#
C#	A#

Major Key (Flats)	Relative Minor
F	Dm
Bb	G
Eb	C
Ab	F
Db	Bb
Gb	Eb
Cb	Ab

The next type of minor scale is the **melodic minor**. This is the simplest minor scale that is possible. It is a major scale with a *b3*.

Major scale: A-B-C#-D-E-F#-G#

Melodic minor scale: A-B-C-D-E-F#-G#

In the musical world, the melodic minor is played ascending only, and they descend playing the natural minor. This isn't always the case and I don't follow that rule at all, so you don't have to either.

A Melodic Minor

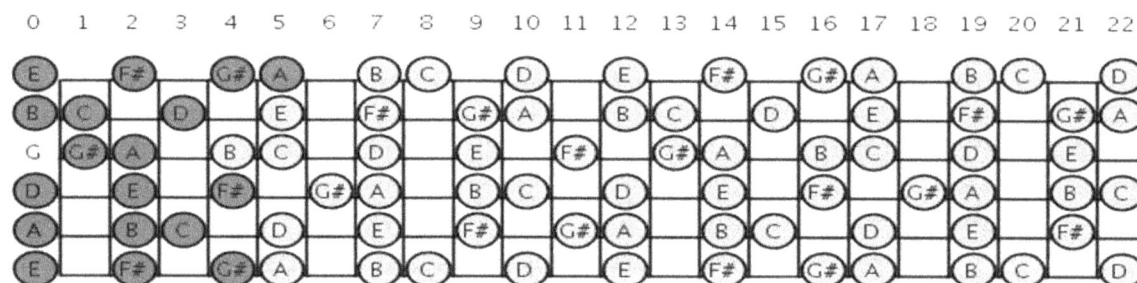

The last of the most common types of minor scales is the **harmonic minor**. There is a bit more to this one than the melodic minor scale. The harmonic minor is used to correct the natural minor's i-iv-v progression. When you play the natural minor's i-iv-v progression, there is a touch of tension on the v chord. By raising the third and making a V chord (major not minor), the progression has better harmony, hence the name harmonic minor. Try playing a passage using the 1-4-5 chords from the natural minor and then the harmonic minor. Two progressions in Am are below.

Natural Minor: i-iv-v = Am-Dm-Em

Harmonic Minor: i-iv-V = Am-Dm-E

You will notice that the E major chord at the end of the harmonic minor progression sounds, well more harmonic. The chords built out of the natural minor (like we do with the major scale) are identical to that of the major scale. That's because they are essentially the same scale. The chords built from the other minors (why anyone would make a chord progression from this scale is beyond me) are a bit more interesting than from the natural minor. Note: there are no melodic minor or harmonic minor keys. They share the same key signature as the natural minor scale. But, you can make chords from them if you wish.

Table 10-2 shows the different triads and seventh chords that are built by using the minor scales. They share some similarities and some differences between them. Note that the half-diminished chords show no triads because the terminology is the same.

Table 10-2:

Natural Minor	Am Am7	B°	C Cmaj7	Dm Dm7	Em Em7	F Fmaj7	G G7
Melodic Minor	Am Am(maj7)	Bm Bm7	C Cmaj7#5	D D7	E E7	F#°	G#m G#m♭5
Harmonic Minor	Am Am(maj7)	B°	C Cmaj7#5	D D7	E E7	F°	G#°

The harmonic minor is pretty well known for being a "classical" sounding scale. It has very interesting properties. The harmonic minor has a famous mode (they all have modes) that gets used quite a bit in the neoclassical metal genre. This is the Phrygian dominant scale. It is also referred to as the Spanish Phrygian,

Ahava Rabboh, Freygish, Jewish scale, Hijaz maqam, gypsy scale, Neapolitan minor scale, and who knows what else.

It is essentially the 5th mode of the harmonic minor scale. Where the *A* harmonic minor would read:

A-B-C-D-E-F-G#

The Phrygian dominant scale is:

E-F-G#-A-B-C-D

It is called a dominant scale because it is a major scale (G#) with a *b*7 (D). This is the characteristic of a dominant scale.

E Phrygian Dominant

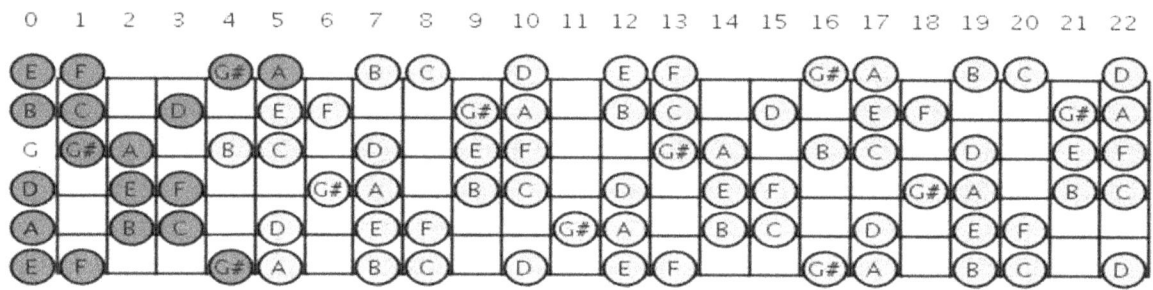

How to use minors:

When playing an Am chord there is the opportunity to play any three of these scales on top of them. Obvious to some, when playing a Am7 you only have one option (of the 3), the natural minor. This is because the other two minors have a *G#* instead of a *G* as the 7th note. You can of course write an entire chord progression to fit a specific minor scale, as well.

Playing a solo in music or an overlaying melody line does not have to be the boring old *C* major scale over a *C* major chord. A *C* major chord has 3 notes in it, *C-E-G*. The 3 chord is an Em chord. If you want, you could play the *E* Phrygian (*C* major scale starting on the *E*) or you could play the *E* natural minor scale (*G* major scale starting on the *E*, remember it is the Aeolian mode). There are two easy options. The melodic and harmonic minors, in Am, won't work because of the *G*.

The cool thing about most rock oriented music (rock, metal, progressive, you get the picture) is that the chords usually come in the format of a 5 chord. This is a "chord" that has only the 1 and the 5 played. This of course leaves out the 3 making it have no characteristic of being either major or minor. This allows for many more opportunities to play things that you wouldn't play on top of regular triads or greater.

Think about it. You only have to stay in the realm of music that is being played. If the bass is playing an E note, and the rhythm guitar is playing an E5 chord (E-B) then you can play anything that doesn't have an E*b* or B*b* in it, basically. I play like this. For instance, the E5 chord is strummed. Do I need to play an E natural minor scale because I know the song is in *G*? Of course not. I could, if I wanted to, play an E major scale, because it would fit. Then on the next chord, change keys, scales, modes, or arpeggios as the next chord deems appropriate.

This may sound illogical, because of keys. I play in a way that I believe opens up the song, not in a way that is stifled by theory. I use theory to my advantage, not the other way around. Knowing the notes of chords, knowing the notes in a scale, and using them where they fit are what matters. Don't limit yourself. I was talking to a very musically intelligent violin instructor one day. I asked him about Mozart. I asked, "Why does he play these weird notes here and there that are out of key?" He replied, "Because it sounds good". There is no theory do describe taste, flavor, or avant-garde. Theory is used to give a reason behind why music sounds good, and to assist in the creation and understanding of music.

The key to using any form of theory is to just try it, play it, understand it, and make plenty of mistakes. One chord can have many, many different scales played on top of it depending on what sound you want. Experiment. Use different methods, different scales, etc. The relative minor is the easiest way to start. Take the *C* major scale. Simply play an *A* natural minor scale over the chord. It's that easy. You understand why you could do that, right?

Chapter 11
Theory Outro

Remember, as you finish this book that this is in no way exhaustive. I assure you many will be exhausted reading this, but it doesn't cover all scopes of theory. There is much more to be discussed and explained, but that's another book entirely. This book has attempted to give you the understanding of theory, foundations of theory, and in a way, the principles of theory.

I would encourage you to take formal lessons if you aren't already doing so right now. I always, in my teaching career, intended on creating musicians as opposed to guitar players. The world of music is vast and if you don't capitalize on the theory behind it you'll be playing in the sandbox while others are at the beach.

Don't place value on tabs and licks. While these are good things to apply, they are in no way a cheat for true knowledge. I tried to stay away from a lot of exercises, because usually all someone will do is thumb to the tab, play it, and close the book. That isn't what this is about.

I believe that everybody can learn theory. The people who can't, won't. If that makes any sense. What I am saying is that if you need to ask a question, ask someone who teaches for a living. If they don't know, e-mail a music professor at a college or university. If they don't answer, because they think they're above the question, and usually they do, write another professor somewhere else, or call the music teacher at a local school. If you want to know, you will get the information you desire.

If you take the time to learn these concepts you will come to see that the music community is theory dumb. This is a sad, sad thing. How can 90% of musicians not know what they are doing after 10 or 20 years? In some conversations there might be a time when I mention that I play the guitar, and I feel let down because they believe that I play like every other dude out there. I should say from now on that I am a musician and I play the guitar, but that sounds rather stupid.

You know what chaps my butt more than a snow cone 3 foot high? A pianist that believes the guitar isn't a classical instrument. I know many pianists who, when you tell them that you are a guitarist, tend to look down their nose at you. I hate to break it to them, but the piano has only been around since the 1700's. The guitar on the other hand has been around, in one form or another, since the early Biblical times. It is the lack of knowledgeable guitarists that gives the impression that if you are a guitarist, you are musically ignorant. So buck up! You represent a greater whole.

I encourage you to write music down. Learn notation. If you learn basic theory, notation is a breeze. It is the easy way to write what we have learned throughout this book. The internet can be a fine source of information, but on the other hand it can be knowledge written by fools. Be very careful where you get your theory info from. Use caution and substantiate the information.

With that I bid you adieu. I hope that you close this book with more knowledge that you started it with. It is in my most desirable wishes that you become the best guitarist/musician that you can be and that you continue this journey seeking to understand music more. God bless!

Bryan DeLauney

www.ingramcontent.com/pod-product-compliance
Lightning Source LLC
Chambersburg PA
CBHW081519040426
42447CB00013B/3271